D1301918

FLUCTUATIONS IN GENERAL BUSINESS

Fluctuations

In

General

Business

By

Montgomery D. Anderson, Ph.D.

and

Ralph H. Blodgett, Ph.D.

THE CHRISTOPHER PUBLISHING HOUSE
NORTH QUINCY, MASS. 02171

PRINTED IN
THE UNITED STATES OF AMERICA

To Our Beloved Sons and Daughters

"All great truths begin as blasphemies"
George Bernard Shaw

CONTENTS

3

LIST OF FIGURES

LIST OF TABLES

FLUCTUATIONS IN GENERAL BUSINESS

Chapter 1

INTRODUCTION

In view of the serious consequences which booms and recessions bring to large numbers of people, it is not surprising that the task of finding an explanation of these fluctuations in general business has engaged the attention of a large number of economists (and also airline pilots, physicists, newspaper writers, television stars, and almost everyone) for many years. And most analysts have been committed to the idea that booms and depressions are parts of a mechanism known as the "business cycle." According to this notion, the various phases or periods of the business cycle follow each other in unending succession and with considerable regularity, and each cycle is similar to other cycles to such an extent that one may hope to find some single explanation for all of them.

Many economists have developed rather standardized descriptions of the typical business cycle which attempt to show what happens in each of the phases or periods, such as prosperity, crisis, depression, and recovery. In practice, however, it is frequently difficult or impossible to identify these periods and it is necessary to confine attention to just the upward and downward movements in general business activity, which are often called periods of business expansion and contraction.

Even such periods show considerable variation from one case to another. Upward movements, downward movements, and complete upward and downward movements differ greatly in duration. Moreover, the upward movement has sometimes been several times as long as the downward movement, while in other cases exactly the reverse has been true. Equally large variations have occurred in the amplitude or severity of the upward and downward movements. And each period of business expansion or contraction is likely to contain some factors or features peculiar to itself.

Because of such considerations, some economists doubt whether there is any such thing as a business cycle, as the term is generally understood. Most economists conclude, however, that periods of general business expansion and contraction and the turning points between them can be readily identified, and that it should be possible to discover some generalized explanation of these fluctuations in total economic activity.

The theories which have been developed to explain cyclical fluctuations in general business activity are both numerous and varied. Some theories have depended on factors external to the economic system, such as sunspot cycles, eight-year cycles of the planet Venus, gold discoveries, changes in population and migration, waves of scientific and technological discoveries and innovations, and wars, revolutions, and political developments. Some of these "external" factors are clearly independent of the economic system, but in other cases it seems likely that there may be interaction between the economic system and the so-called outside factors.

Other theories have relied upon factors internal to the economic system and have stressed the expansion and contraction of bank credit, alternating waves of optimism and pessimism on the part of the business community, overproduction or underconsumption, and many other things. Still other theories have attempted a synthesis of these internal and external factors. Some of the theories had relatively few followers and some had many, but for many years no single theory came close to being generally accepted by economists.

This situation has changed in the last few decades. The explanation of fluctuations in general economic activity developed by the English economist, John Maynard Keynes (later Lord Keynes) in his book *The General Theory of Employment, Interest, and Money* (1936), and by his followers, now seems to be accepted by the great bulk of economists. This theory emphasizes changes in the level of total spending, as determined by the interaction of the monetary forces of saving and investment.

Saving, it is said, occurs when people (natural or corporate) receive money income and do not spend it. Investment, on the other hand, refers to the expenditure of money income to acquire new capital goods (not existing capital goods or the securities and other paper items which represent them). The equilibrium level of the national income is that at which people who save are willing to save exactly the same aggregate sum as those who invest are willing to invest.

However, there is no guarantee that, in an existing situation, all the people in the economy will want to save exactly the same total amount as that which they will want to invest. It is recognized that some saving is done by the same people who will invest the saved funds, but the theory holds that saving and investment are processes which are carried on to a considerable extent by different groups of people and for largely different reasons. Large numbers of people save; they save for many and varied reasons, and many of the reasons are not at all closely connected with the interest rate. Total saving is related to the level of national income in a passive way and depends upon individual propensities to consume and save at various levels of income.

Investment is carried on by businessmen, and investing is done when potentially profitable investment opportunities are deemed to exist. Investment is thus said to depend upon the relationship of the marginal efficiency of capital to the rate of interest. The existence of attractive investment opportunities depends upon dynamic and rather unpredictable factors of growth in the economic system, and upon such other things as technology, government taxation and expenditure policies, legislative activities, and optimistic and pessimistic expectations. Investment is a volatile thing, and the amount of investing which businessmen want to do is capable of great variation from one period of time to another.

National income (and production and employment) must always adjust to such a level that the total sum which the people of the economy want to save is equal to that which businessmen want to invest. If, in a given situation, the people of the economy want to save a greater total sum than that which businessmen want to invest, the level of national income must fall until these two important economic aggregates become equal. And, conversely, if businessmen try to invest a greater total sum than that which the people of the economy are willing to save in a given situation, the national income must rise until total saving and total investment become equal.

It is also to be noted that increases in national income, production and employment may tend to induce additional investment beyond that originally contemplated by businessmen. Such increases in investment are judged to have a multiplied effect on national income, and the concept of the "multiplier" or "investment multiplier" is developed. The multiplier is a numerical coefficient which shows how great an increase in national income may be expected to occur as the result of a given increase in investment. Thus, if an increase of five billion dollars in investment caused an increase of 20 billion dollars in national income, the multiplier would be four. The multiplier is considered to be the reciprocal of the economy's marginal propensity to save. Declines in total investment are also said to have a multiplied effect in reducing the national income.

Many versions of the theory under discussion include another concept called the acceleration principle. This principle holds that changes in the production of capital goods, or producers' goods, are dependent with respect to both amplitude and timing on the changes which occur in the production (and sale) of consumers' goods. In a particular industry, if the production and sale of consumers' goods in a period of business expansion continue to grow but at a slower rate than formerly, the industry's demand for new capital equipment actually tends to decline. And, if the production of consumers' goods becomes stabilized at a high level or declines a little, the industry's demand for new capital equipment tends to disappear completely for the time being.

The changes in the production of capital goods not only occur *when* the rate of production of the relevant consumers' goods changes but also are much greater relatively than those which take place in the output of consumers' goods. That is, a decline of 10 percent in the output of consumers' goods may produce a decline of 100 percent in the production of the machines and equipment necessary to the production of the particular final products. Moreover, declines in the production of capital goods (and in investment in these goods) will tend to produce magnified effects on the national income, as indicated above.

The theory under discussion holds that the total employment of labor is a direct function of the total national income and production, and is independent of changes in money wage rates and the money prices of goods. In a period of business contraction, cuts in money wage rates will prove futile as a means of increasing total employment. In fact, some writers contend that cuts in money wage rates may affect total employment adversely, but this would seem to be mathematically impossible if total employment is independent of changes in money wage rates and money prices of goods. In any case, cuts in money wage rates could help only if they had some favorable effect on the marginal propensity to consume, the marginal efficiency of capital, or the rate of interest, and such effects are deemed unlikely.

In the absence of such effects, money prices are likely to fall as much as money wage rates are cut, so that real wages are as high as ever. Businessmen, although helped by lower costs as the result of reduced money wage rates, are harmed to an equal degree when lower total money wages are spent by a large segment of the consuming population. Thus, cuts in money wage rates in a period of business contraction tend to be self-defeating.

Since the theory of business fluctuations under discussion stresses changes in the level of total spending as determined by the monetary forces of saving and investment, it must be concerned in some degree with changes in the total supply of money. However, the old theory, sometimes called the "quantity theory of money," which held that the level of total spending and of prices is directly proportional to the size of the available money supply, was no longer held strongly. It was noted that prices do not always change directly in proportion to total spending, and that total spending itself is not likely to change directly in proportion to changes in the total money supply because of variability in the velocity of circulation or rate of turnover of money.

It came to be held that an increase in the amount of money available in the economy tends to lower the rate of interest. When the interest rate falls and increased credit is available, the volume of spending for investment is likely to increase, and this development tends to increase national income, production, and employment. Of course, if increases in production were not easily possible, much of the effect might be on prices rather than on production. This whole mechanism will also operate in the reverse direction.

Thus the objective of monetary policy would be to move the economy's investment schedule up or down so that the level of national income at which total investment is equal to total saving will be at or near the full-employment level and at stable prices. It is recognized, however, that changes in the amount of money may not affect the interest rate strongly and that changes in the rate of interest may not influence greatly the rate of spending for investment. A decline in the rate of interest from 6 percent to 4 percent is not likely to increase the rate of investment spending of a businessman who expects to make minus 10 percent a year from an investment in new capital goods.

The interest rate is thought of as the price which is paid for the use of money. The equilibrium rate of interest must be such that the people of the economy as a whole want to hold precisely the total quantity of money which is available for them to hold. If the interest rate were higher, people would not want to hold all of the available stock of money but would prefer to put their money into securities and other types of assets which are less liquid than money. However, in this case the prices of securities and other assets would rise and their effective rates of return would decline until people once more wanted to hold all of the money available.

In the opposite case, people would want to hold more than the total available stock of money if the rate of interest obtainable in less liquid uses of funds were too low. However, in this case the prices of securities and other assets would tend to fall and their effective rates of return would rise until people once more wanted to hold only the total amount of money available for them to hold.

Although not required to do so by the theory itself, most economists who hold to the theory of business fluctuations under discussion believe that the government should step in and use its fiscal policy to correct a situation in which there is an important discrepancy between the total saving intended by the people of the economy and the total investment which businessmen want to maintain. By increasing its expenditures without increasing its income or by increasing its income without increasing its expenditures, the government is supposed to be able to correct either a deflationary or an inflationary gap between the total amount which people are intending to spend for consumption and investment and the amount which needs to be spent if the economy is to operate at a full-employment level of production and national income.

The national income which is so important in this analysis can be measured in practice from either of two points of view. On the one hand, national income should be the total costs of the output of services and tangible goods payable as earnings to the owners of the productive agents. On the other hand, national income should be equal to the total net value of the services and tangible goods produced by these agents.

It is actually rather difficult to get the two estimates of national income to agree. From the product side, it is customary to start with gross national product, or the market value of the economy's entire output of final commodities and services in a given period. A figure for gross national product is reached by adding estimates for personal consumption expenditures, gross private domestic investment, net foreign investment, and government purchases of goods and services.

It is next recognized that gross national product does not give us a satisfactory measure of the net contribution of the productive system to the volume of goods available for consumption and to the economy's total stock of capital goods. The reason is that all capital goods produced in the given period are counted in gross national product whether they represent a net increase in the stock of capital goods or merely go to replace others which, for one reason or another, have become or are becoming no longer useful. Therefore, gross national product is next converted into what is called net national product by deducting a capital consumption allowance, which consists for the most part of a rather arbitrary estimate of the depreciation of durable capital goods, from gross national product.

Even the resulting figure for net national product is not nearly the same as that for national income which is arrived at on the basis of the earnings of the productive agents. However, the two figures are made to agree by deducting from net national product some further amounts which represent indirect business taxes, business transfer payments, net government subsidies, and an interesting little item called "statistical discrepancy."

The theory of fluctuations in total economic activity developed by Lord Keynes and his followers has been variously evaluated by different writers. To many, Keynes was a many-sided genius whose work produced the greatest revolution in economic thinking in modern times and is likely to be regarded as a classic for generations to come. On the other hand, one writer, after a careful and detailed analysis of the *General Theory,* reported that he could not "find in it a single important doctrine that is both true and original. What is original in the book is not true; and what is true is not original. In fact. . .even much that is fallacious is not original, but can be found in a score of previous writers." Moreover, the book contains "an incredible number of fallacies, inconsistencies, vaguenesses, shifting definitions and usages of words, and plain errors of fact."[1]

In the present work, our primary purpose is not to demolish or even to criticize any economist or his works. When Keynesian concepts seem ambiguous or otherwise poorly suited to analytical pur-

---

[1] Henry Hazlitt, *The Failure of the "New Economics."* Princeton: D. Van Nostrand Company, 1959, pp. 6-7.

poses or when conclusions usually drawn by the Keynesian analysis seem to be invalid, we will not hesitate to say so. But our main objective is to present a new theory of fluctuations in total economic activity based upon the use of mathematics, statistics, accounting, economic analysis, and (we hope) common sense.

Chapter 2

FLUCTUATIONS IN THE TOTAL FLOW
OF FUNDS AS REFERENCE CYCLES

Explanations of business cycles, and especially those which make extensive use of statistical analysis, often employ the concept of a standard cycle or "reference cycle" in general economic activity, to which fluctuations in important variables may be related. It seems clear to us that the most useful reference cycles for a study of fluctuations in the major economic aggregates are the changes which occur in the total flow of funds in exchange for services and tangible goods, taken without regard to any statistical adjustment for trend.

Such reference cycles will clearly include fluctuations other than the purely cyclical, and we shall be stretching the usual nomenclature of business cycle analysis in giving this name to changes in the raw data for the flow of funds. On the other hand, by using the raw data on the flow of funds we shall avoid all wishful statistical operations in the fitting of trends; that is, statistical adjustments which might be designed unwittingly to produce close correlations which could not be duplicated if other trends were used and which would not stand up in other periods of time on the basis of extrapolations of the trends actually used.

Moreover, the relationships which the businessman needs most urgently to understand are relationships between the *whole* behavior of various factors in the business cycle. If an exact (or nearly exact) and reliable statement of the whole behavior of the important factors in the business cycle can be given, the individual businessman or the individual student of business cycles will then be free to apply to such total behavior any secular trends which he considers most suitable for his purpose. He would thereby arrive at the "pure cycles" by eliminating the secular trend and other components of behavior in the raw data which are foreign to the "pure cycle."

The concept of a pure cycle is a useful one for some purposes, but it is after all a figment of the human imagination, whereas the total behavior of business aggregates is something which may be regarded as objective and concrete. So long as there is so much misunderstanding of the total behavior of business aggregates which needs to be cleared up, we do not want to assume the burden of defining in theory and locating in practice the purely cyclical part of the total behavior.

This analysis will be concerned almost entirely with the relationships which must obtain between the total fluctuations of business aggregates. Therefore we choose changes in the unadjusted data for the total flow of funds as our reference cycles in the sense that we intend to refer the raw fluctuations of many other business aggregates to changes in the raw data for the total flow of funds. It may not be strictly accurate to apply the term "reference cycles" to changes in the total flow of funds. A more precise designation would be "reference fluctuations." However, this term has a pedantic sound, and the other term, "reference cycles," has been well known for many years since it was popularized by Dr. Wesley C. Mitchell. (See Arthur F. Burns and Wesley C. Mitchell, *Measuring Business Cycles.* New York: National Bureau of Economic Research, 1946, p. 24.)

If it is understood that we are going to be concerned with unadjusted data, why do we consider it obvious that changes in the total flow of funds are the best choice for reference cycles? This decision was based upon a number of considerations. Almost any analysis is certain to be interested in the relationship of the parts of a whole to the whole, and the total flow of funds is equal to the sum of all the monetary transactions in a given economy in a given period of time.

The total flow of funds includes many of the other important aggregates in the theory of business fluctuations, such as total wages and salaries, total interest and rents paid, total taxes paid (construed as payments for the services of government), total purchases of so-called capital goods, total new income, and, as will be shown, total savings (construed as a negative item). The total flow of funds embraces these important sub-aggregates in all sectors of the economy— corporate, individual, partnership, and governmental. A payment of taxes to the government is included, as is the purchase of an atomic missile by the government. Finally, the total flow of funds includes all monetary transactions in an interval of time, regardless of whether they involve the immediate payment of money itself.

In order that the concept of the total flow of funds may be understood clearly, let us define what we mean by "funds." As a first approximation, funds may be said to be "real" accounts in the language of accounting, in which a real account is any account which appears in the balance sheet or financial statement. Positively-valued funds are all those asset accounts which are not tangible assets. In short, positively-valued funds are simply the dollar value of such intangible assets as cash, bank deposits receivable, accounts receivable, bonds and mortgages owned, as well as preferred and common stock owned.

A flow of funds, as we define it, occurs whenever some tangible asset or some service is obtained by an exchange in which a positively-valued fund is reduced at some point in the economy, or when a negatively-valued fund is increased. Thus there is a flow of funds when an individual buys a pair of shoes for cash. His positively-valued funds are reduced by an amount equal to the price of the shoes. The same is true if he acquires a piece of real estate in exchange for government bonds.

As just indicated, there are negatively-valued funds as well as positively-valued funds, and the purchase of a tangible good or service may be paid for by an *increase* in the value of the buyer's supply of negatively-valued funds. Negatively-valued funds are simply the value of all liabilities in the broad sense of the word which includes equitable as well as legal obligations. Or it may be said that the total value of negatively-valued funds is equal to the sum of all the real accounts on the right-hand side of the balance sheet.

Funds are negative when regarded from the point of view of the person to whom they represent an obligation and they are positive from the point of view of the beneficiary of the obligation. For example, a promissory note is a positively-valued fund to the holder but a negatively-valued fund (or note payable) to the debtor. Negative funds include accounts payable, notes payable, and preferred or common stock appearing on the right-hand side of the balance sheet. An apparent exception to this distinction based on point of view would be gold coins, which are positively-valued funds to their owner but which are not negatively valued by anybody. This very minor exception to the rule of equality may be removed from logical consideration altogether by holding that gold coins are not funds at all, but rather tangible assets.

If you acquire a pair of shoes by increasing your accounts payable (i.e., by "charging" the purchase), there is a flow of funds from you to the shoe store, which is a negative flow from your point of view but a positive flow (an increase of accounts receivable) to the shoe store. If you acquire a locomotive by issuing equipment trust certificates, there is also a flow of funds, which are negative from the point of view of the issuing railroad but which are positively-valued to the bank which buys the certificate.

Since the same flow of funds may appear to involve positively-valued funds from one point of view and negatively-valued from another, it is clear that the total flow of positively-valued funds in the entire economy is always equal to the total flow of negatively-valued funds. But it is important to note that we do not include both flows when we compile the aggregate flow of funds in an economy for a given period of time. One or the other is always counted, but not both.

When positively-valued funds are exchanged directly for negatively-valued funds, we have a transaction which does not represent the purchase and sale of any tangible good or service, and so we do not include the flow in either direction in our concept of the aggregate flow of funds. It simplifies the mathematics of the interrelation of factors in the total volume of business to make this exclusion. Thus we would not include in the total flow of funds a transaction in which a promissory note is exchanged for a check drawn on a bank. This kind of transaction may *imply* the existence of a service, but it does not in and of itself register the value of such service. On the other hand, when a borrower gives a check to a lender to compensate him for the *use* of funds, we include the transaction because the use of funds is a kind of service.

In order to avoid the repetition of a cumbersome expression, we shall henceforth speak of "the total flow of funds" instead of "the total flow of funds in exchange for tangible goods and services." The only exceptions will be found in cases where the qualifying phrase is needed in order to emphasize the distinction which is being made at the time.

For the economy as a whole all of the business aggregates which represent the movement of goods and services between traders are a part of the total flow of funds. These business aggregates are in accounting parlance the "nominal" accounts; that is to say, they do not appear as such in the financial statement but rather in the statement of income from operations (the income statement). The nominal accounts for the economy as a whole are related to the total flow of funds by simple addition or subtraction. When the books are cleared for the period, the net effect of the nominal accounts on the "real" accounts is reckoned, and here again the relationship is a matter of simple addition or subtraction.

But the "real" accounts themselves, as conceived in economics, (that is, total capital, increase of capital, total stock of funds, and total savings, for example) are not all related to the total flow of funds by simple addition or subtraction. However, we expect to demonstrate that most real account aggregates can be expressed as fairly simple functions of the total flow of funds and a few other variables which do not appear explicitly in either the national balance sheet or the national statement of income from operations.

Changes in the total flow of funds are our choice as reference "cycles" because it is possible to relate all of the important national accounts, both real[1] and nominal to the total flow of funds. That is to say, the behavior of most aggregate accounts, real or nominal, may be explained in terms of our reference cycles and a bare minimum of other variables. But to explain the behavior of each factor in the business cycle in terms of a generalized system of concepts is to relate the behavior of any one factor to that of all of the others. As a result we are able to construct a rather complete model of endogenous relationships in the interaction of factors in the so-called business cycle—except for the purely financial factors which we have perforce omitted from our model when we excluded purely financial barter from our concept of the total flow of funds.

If it be suggested that we in effect propose to put on a production of *Hamlet* without the prince of Denmark, we reply that we are not going to eliminate the effects of financial activity on the production of tangible goods and services by any means. We might also add in our rebuttal that a complete theory of business fluctuations has not yet been written and probably never will be written.

We also propose to omit from our model such exogenous factors as

---

[1] The reader must bear in mind that the accounting concept of a "real" account is entirely different from the economic concept. In accounting parlance, "real" variables have nothing to do with the price level, and a "real" account does not mean a variable which has been "deflated" or corrected for changes in the value or purchasing power of the dollar.

wars, crop failures, central bank policy, and the fiscal policy of the federal government. These exogenous factors have a teriffic effect on total business activity but, whatever the impact may be, it cannot disturb the endogenous relationships between the national aggregates which we propose to derive. This is so because the relationships in which we are primarily interested are either mathematical identities or quasi-identities which must obtain, subject to only a few broad and reliable statistical assumptions.

Indeed, the model which we propose to construct is non-parametric with respect to the dominant type of economic organization within a country so long as there is a widespread division of labor and a monetary valuation of practically all transactions. Whether the increase of capital is owned by individuals or by the state, it has a necessary relation to the increase of total wages and certain other factors, and it does not matter whether the employees are working for private persons and firms for the most part as is the case in the United States or are working for the state as is the case in Soviet Russia. In short, our model will be relevant to an understanding of total economic behavior in an economic system marked by state control in an extreme form or in the modified form which has been superimposed upon free enterprise in this country.

It is important to observe that the total flow of funds is known by several other names in the language of the theory of business fluctuations. Some of these other names were used rather commonly before the Board of Governors of the Federal Reserve System christened this aggregate as the total flow of funds. In the first place the total flow of funds, as we use the term, is equal to the total purchases of services and tangible goods in the economy (plus purchases from the rest of the world, if it is desired to include them) *valued at cost to the buyers.* Secondly, the total flow of funds is equal to the total sales of tangible goods and services, again valued at cost to the buyers. In the third place, the total flow of funds is equal to the total input of services and tangible goods to all firms, if all firms are considered as producing units (and therefore as having inputs and outputs of goods and services) and if "firms" are taken to include all natural persons, whether farmers or not, all corporations, and all units of government.

A part of this last consideration is not entirely in accord with conventional thinking because most people would not consider an ordinary working man, who is not a farmer, to be a firm. Nevertheless, he is a producing unit and he has an input of commodities and services out of which he derives the physical, mental, and emotional powers to produce by his labors that which may be regarded as his output. Even if he is paid by the hour for his services, there exists for him a balance sheet and a statement of income from operations, whether or not he is aware of their existence.

An ordinary working man may not keep personal bookkeeping records, but we as economists and national accountants may keep the records for him in the aggregate. During any year he has a certain outflow of funds and in return he receives certain inputs, such as food, clothing, fuel, and even recreation, which enable him to maintain a certain output of (say) so many bricks laid in construction work. We may regard him as a one-man entrepreneur or firm, and we are entitled to speak of his input and output, and of the net difference which represents the gain or loss in his tangible capital. Any worker falls in essentially the same category with respect to input-output analysis as the independent farmer, who has long been regarded by economists and statisticians as a producing unit or one-man firm.[2]

Of course, in order to maintain our concept of total input we shall have to treat a rich playboy as a producing unit even though his input may contain unusual amounts of caviar and champagne and his output consists largely of headlines for the edification of the masses in the popular news media. However, any statistical discrepancy or departure from reality caused by such distortions of common sense will be very small in relation to the total flow of funds, and the gain in terms of simplicity of analysis will outweigh the loss in terms of departure from common sense.

Subject to the stated understanding, then, we may say that the total outflow of funds (that is, the sum of the decreases of positive funds and/or increases of negative funds) is equal to (a) total purchases of services and tangible goods, (b) the total inflow of funds, and (c) the total input of tangible goods and services into all of the producing units of the economy.

For every individual firm an outflow of funds (positive or negative) in exchange for tangible goods gives rise to two entries of equal dollar value on its books, (1) a credit to funds and (2) a debit to

---

[2] For that matter, the various divisions of government have not always been regarded as producing units, and there are some willful cynics who would still deny that government is productive.

purchases of tangible goods. The term "purchases" is used here in a general sense rather than a narrow technical sense. It is understood that "fixed" capital assets acquired would be debited to a capital account rather than to an account labeled "purchases." Such assets are not usually resold directly by the purchaser and user and therefore do not normally appear in the output account labeled "sales." Nevertheless they appear constructively as a part of output—or expense—as they wear out and are charged off to depreciation. When they are depreciated to zero they may be said to be completely "sold" or completely "turned over" as a part of the "output" during the period over which the total depreciation occurred. Since this is true for each firm, it is true for all firms taken together, and the real or constructive output of tangible goods and services for society as a whole is equal to the total inflow of funds in exchange therefor, when the outflow of tangible goods and services is valued at cost to the buyers.

Thus, the total input of goods and services at any given time, valued at cost to the buyers, is equal to the total outflow of funds, and the total output of goods and services valued at cost to the buyers is equal as well to the total inflow of funds. The outflow of goods and services at such valuation is also equal to the total inflow of funds at the given time. These equalities do not prevent the realization of an increase of capital over a period of time because the total profit for the given period is equal to the difference between output at one time and the output at another or earlier time, as we propose to show in this study.

The essential thing to be emphasized at this stage of the analysis is that for the economy as a whole—which includes all buyers as well as all sellers—there are at least six different names for the same statistical entity, viz.

(1) Total outflow of funds for services and tangible goods at a given time.

(2) Total inflow of funds at the same time.

(3) Total purchases of goods and services at the same time, valued at cost to the buyers.

(4) Total sales of goods and services at the same time, valued at cost to the buyers.

(5) Total input valued in the same way at the same time.

(6) Total output valued in the same way at the same time.

The multiple names for the same statistical identity do not however constitute a redundancy or plethora of language, for each designation carries a somewhat different connotation in conception.

It is important to fix these six identities for the economy as a whole clearly in mind because, in the course of the argument, it will sometimes be more revealing or meaningful to use one name, and sometimes another, and sometimes even to use two or more names at the same time. It should also be noted that our reference cycles may be given by the changes in any one of the six concepts or ways of labeling the same statistical aggregate, measured in dollar value in this country.

Books of account furnish us with accumulations of the flow of funds over finite intervals of time ending at specific points in time, as, for example, the twelve months ending on December 31, 1940. We shall designate such a statistical datum by the symbol Z_τ, meaning the total sales of services and tangible goods during some finite period of time ending at time $t = \tau$, wherein t is ordered time in general and τ is a particular value of t. Notwithstanding the fact that the available data are accumulations over intervals of time, in the mathematical argument it will be less cumbersome to work out the relationship between instantaneous rates at given moments rather than with accumulations over intervals of time. Then we can integrate our equations for a finite interval of time equal to the accounting period and compare these definite integrals with the actual statistical evaluations which are available on the books of account. We shall therefore prefer to develop our mathematical analysis in terms of the total rate of sales (or purchases) considered as a function of time in general, and we shall give this concept the symbol $Z(t)$.

It follows at once that Z_τ is the definite integral of $Z(t)$ from time $t = \tau$ back to time $t = \tau - \epsilon$, where ϵ is any given finite period of time, or

$$Z_\tau \equiv \int_{\tau-\epsilon}^{\tau} Z(t)dt. \qquad\qquad 2:1$$

In much of our statistical work we shall take ϵ to be one year, but this is only a matter of statistical adaptation. In general, the duration of ϵ does not affect the argument and may in theory be taken to be any finite interval of time whatsoever.[3]

---

[3]Since the available statistical data are all for accumulations, Z_τ the values of Z in practice would have to be inferred by some process of interpolation among the known values of Z_τ. However, that detail need not concern us at this point. We assume throughout this work that for society as a whole there does exist in fact an instantaneous rate of flow of funds which is a continuous function of time having continuous derivatives.

Approximate values for Z_T in the United States for the period 1939-1954 inclusive may be obtained from the *Federal Reserve Bulletin* for October, 1955;[4] and approximate values for the same aggregate for the years from 1919 to 1932 from R. R. Doane's *Measurement of American Wealth.*[5] The gap years of 1933-1938 inclusive may be bridged with some data published by Clark Warburton.[6] As a matter of fact, the Doane data themselves go back to 1911, but there is some question of their reliability prior to 1919. In the end, we have fairly good approximations of Z_T for the United States for a continuous period of 36 years.

It is important to note that, while the numerical value of $Z(t)$ for the middle of any given year may be fairly close to the numerical value of Z_T for that year, the *dimensions* of $Z(t)$ and Z_T are quite different. The dimension of $Z(t)$ is billions of dollars per year (as measured in our tables given below), whereas the dimension of Z_T is just plain billions of dollars.

Even the Federal Reserve data seem to us to be only approximations of Z_T. This is not because of the inevitable errors of omission and compilation in census-taking. Such errors are to some extent compensatory and tend to cancel out. Rather the data seem to be only approximations because of the inclusion of an item which does not belong in the total flow of funds.

Let us refer for the sake of illustration to the tableau for 1940 on page 1108 of the *Federal Reserve Bulletin* for October, 1955 (shown here as Table 1). The table is divided dichotomously with respect to financial and nonfinancial flow of funds. It is the nonfinancial (that is, the flow of funds for things apart from other funds) in which we are interested. Among the stubs, lines A, B, C, D, and I are properly included as elements in the total flow of funds in exchange for services and tangible goods. These cover payroll (personal services), payments on investment (services of capital), insurance and grants, taxes (services of government), and purchases of other goods and services. Lines G and H also belong because they are purchases of capital goods not included in line I.

---

[4]See the "tableaux economiques" appearing on pp. 1107-1122 of the stated issue. Values for 1955 and 1956 are obtainable in the issue of the *Bulletin* for October, 1957, pp. 1191-1192.

[5]New York: Harper and Brothers, 1933, p. 39.

[6]See "The Secular Trend in Monetary Velocity," *Quarterly Journal of Economics,* February, 1949, Table 1, p. 72. Estimates of governmental expenditures for goods have been added to the Warburton data by the present authors.

TABLE 1
SUMMARY OF FLOW-OF-FUNDS ACCOUNTS FOR 1940
S = Sources of Funds, U = Uses of Funds
(Annual flows, in billions of dollars)

Sectors / Transactions	Consumer S	Consumer U	Corporate S	Corporate U	Non-corporate S	Non-corporate U	Farm S	Farm U	Federal S	Federal U	St. and loc. S	St. and loc. U	Banking S	Banking U	Insurance S	Insurance U	Other S	Other U	Rest of the world S	Rest of the world U	Total S	Total U
Nonfinancial																						
A Payroll	49.1	1.0		29.7		6.8		.8		4.0		4.3		.6		.8				1.1	49.1	49.1
B Receipts from and payments on investment	19.9	6.3	4.9	10.1	7.3	13.2	.4	3.8	2.1	1.3	.2	.9	2.0	.8	1.4	4.1	1.6	.4	.2	.6	37.4	37.4
C Insurance and grants	6.7	6.7	.3	2.6	.3	2.5	.6	.1	5.3	3.0	4.1	4.5	.1	.1	6.7	4.2	1.3	.2	.3	.1	22.4	22.5
D Taxes and tax refunds	*	3.1	.1	7.1	.4	2.4		1.3	5.3	1.0	8.1	1.7		.1	*	*	.2				13.4	13.4
E Capital acquisitions	3.7	13.9	8.0	8.0		2.4	-.1	1.3	.1	1.0		1.7										
F Net change in inventories		*.9*		*1.0*		*.3*		*1.0*														
G New fixed capital		*4.5*		*6.3*		*2.1*																
H Other capital acquisitions	*3.7*	*4.5*	*.1*	*.1*	*.4*	*.4*	*-.1*		*.1*	*1.0*											*213.3*	*214.1*
I Purchases and sales of other goods and services		48.1	139.7	88.5	53.6	35.8	8.1	2.9	.7	1.3	1.8	2.3	.3	.2	.2	1.0	.2	1.2	3.4	.8		
J Total	79.4	79.1	145.0	146.1	61.5	61.3	9.1	9.3	8.6	10.6	14.3	13.7	2.3	1.8	8.4	6.3	3.3	3.1	3.9	5.3	335.8	336.6
Financial																						
K Currency and deposits	1.1	2.1		2.2		.7		.2	2.3	-.6		.4	6.9	1.4		.3		-.1		.7	6.9	6.1
L Federal obligations		.5		-.2		*		.1				.1		.3		.6		-.1			2.3	2.4
M Mortgages				-.1	-.1		-.1		-.1									.3		-.3	1.0	1.0
N Corporate securities and State and local obligations	.7	-.7		-.1	.3	.1	.4	*	.1	.1	.3	.2	-.1	*	.2	.9	.2	-.3	-.2	-.2	*	*
O Other		.4	-.3	1.9		-.6			.1	1.0			.5	5.7	.2	-.2	.2	.1	-.2	-3.2	3.9	5.0
P Total	1.8	2.4	1.6	3.8	.2	.3	.4	.2	2.5	.4	.3	.7	7.3	7.5	.2	1.9	.2	.2	-.2	-2.8	14.2	14.6
Q Grand total	81.5	81.5	146.6	146.6	61.8	61.8	9.4	9.4	11.0	11.0	14.6	14.6	9.6	9.6	8.6	8.6	3.5	3.5	3.7	3.7	350.3	350.3
Memoranda:																						
R GNP identifiable in J	.7	65.9	.7	8.5		2.6	.2	2.4	1.4	5.9	.3	7.7	*	.4	*		-.1			1.4	97.6	
S Bank credit in P														3.0							3.0	3.0

*Less than 50 million dollars.

1 Financial sources of funds represent net changes in liabilities; financial uses of funds represent net changes in financial assets.

NOTE.—For contents of each line, see notes to summary tables, pp. 1123-24.

However, line F seems to us to indicate some confusion of thought, and it should not be included in the total flow of funds. It evaluates "net changes in inventories," sometimes at cost and sometimes at market prices. Changes in inventories are items which balance the inventory account. The items represent the difference between input and output of circulating tangible goods within a given accounting period. Suppose this difference to be positive in a given case. This means that the input exceeds the output of these goods, and one should not add the difference either to the input to get the total input nor to the output to get the total output. If you add the balancing item to the input, you are guilty of double counting. If you add the balancing item (net change) to the output of circulating goods, you are falsifying the total output by making it seem larger than it really was.

It is improper to add balancing items to either the debit or the credit side of a nominal account in computing the total flows of funds. The entries on one side of the account represent the flows in one direction and the entries on the other side represent flows in the other direction. The difference between the sum of the flows on the one side and the sum of the flows on the other side should not be added to the flows on either side. However, the statistical value of the discrepancy caused by this factor is indeed small in relation to the total flow of funds, and we may regard the grand totals in the Federal Reserve tables as being good approximations of the aggregates in which we are interested. Disregarding statistical discrepancies, the statistical evaluation of Z_T for any given year between 1939 and 1954 is to be found in column U under the caption "Total" in row J of the appropriate table. The value of Z_T for 1940, for example, was approximately 336.6 billion dollars, as shown in Table 1 above.

Chapter 3

THE INCREASE OF WEALTH EXPRESSED AS A FUNCTION OF NEW INCOME AND THE CONSERVATION OF CAPITAL

Let the cost value of all tangible wealth in the economy at a given moment, $t = \tau$, be represented by the symbol $Y(\tau)$, when the total wealth is considered to be a continuous function of time, t. Let $Z(t)$ be the instantaneous rate of purchase of all tangible goods and services at any moment, valued at cost to the buyers. Z is likewise assumed to be a continuous function of ordered time and is likewise assumed to have continuous derivatives.

Under these conditions we may define a third term, $K(\tau)$, by the following identity:

$$Y(\tau) \equiv \int_{\tau - K(\tau)}^{\tau} Z(t) \, dt. \qquad\qquad 3:1$$

This equation states that the value of all tangible wealth at any moment of time, τ, is equal to the definite integral of $Z(t)$ from the moment τ backward in time to some date equal to $\tau - K(\tau)$, where $K(\tau)$ is the interval of integration, or the interval of time necessary to make formula 3:1 a true statement.

A definite integral can be approximated by summation, and so it is easy to express in common-sense terms the truism stated by the formula. Let τ be the present moment, for example. Now start adding the total purchases of services and tangible goods in the economy backwards in time from the present moment. Add yesterday's purchases to today's, and then to that sum add the purchases of the day before yesterday, and so on. Keep on going backward in time until you reach the point in time at which your accumulation of

31

past purchases of tangible wealth is just equal to the total tangible wealth of today. Call that moment in the past at which you stop the additive process $\tau - K(\tau)$. Obviously it will be separated from today by a time interval equal to $K(\tau)$. Obviously, also, the interval $K(\tau)$ is determined by formula 3:1 from the past history or behavior of these total purchases and by the cost value of total wealth at time $t = \tau$. Thus, the concept $K(\tau)$ clearly measures the length of time over which purchases have to be added in order to arrive at a sum equal to the total cost value of tangible wealth at the moment $t = \tau$.

A more useful significance can be given to the concept K if we first derive the meaning of a similar concept K_{ij}, in relation to Y_{ij} and Z_{ij}, wherein these three concepts refer not to aggregates for the whole economy but rather to a particular kind of good, i, in the possession of the jth trader. Then we may invent the identity

$$Y_{ij}(\tau) \equiv \int_{\tau - K_{ij}}^{\tau} Z_{ij}(t) \, dt. \qquad\qquad 3:2$$

In this formula $Y_{ij}(\tau)$ is the value of the ith good in the hands of the jth trader at time τ, Z_{ij} is a possibly discontinuous function of time tracing the history of the jth trader's purchases of the ith good, and K_{ij} is the interval of time which satisfies the equation $(i = 1, 2, 3, \ldots n)$ where there are n kinds of goods and $j = 1, 2, 3, \ldots m$ where there are m traders in the whole economy.

If we now assume that the evaluation of Y_{ij} is made according to the rule of "first in, first out," it is possible to set up a physical experiment which shows that K_{ij} has a highly important meaning; that is, K_{ij} is the length of time which the particle of the ith good which is just being sold has remained in the possession of the jth trader. K_{ij} is therefore the (historical) period of turnover of the ith category of goods in the possession of the jth trader at the moment $t = \tau$.

There are many values of K_{ij} in the whole economy. That is to say, there are many different periods of turnover for all of the various goods in the hands of all of the individual traders. Since $Z(t)$ equals $\sum_{i=1}^{n} \sum_{j=1}^{m} Z_{ij}(t)$ while $Y(\tau)$ equals $\sum_{i=1}^{n} \sum_{j=1}^{m} Y_{ij}(\tau)$, it must follow that K is some kind of average of all the multitudinous values of K_{ij}. It is, in short, an average (historical) period of turnover of all capital in the economy at time $t = \tau$. (Whenever a given trader, j, has a zero stock of the i th good, that good will not be included in averaging the trader's turnover.)   The type of average of the K_{ij}'s which is equal to K can be ascertained.   By the above definitions:

$$Y(\tau) \equiv \int_{\tau - K(\tau)}^{\tau} Z(t)\, dt \equiv \sum_{i=1}^{n} \sum_{j=1}^{m} \int_{\tau - K_{ij}}^{\tau} Z_{ij}(t)\, dt. \qquad 3{:}3$$

Let $K_{ij}(\tau) \equiv K(\tau) + \delta_{ij}$. Then

$$Y(\tau) \equiv \sum_{i=1}^{n} \sum_{j=1}^{m} \left[\int_{\tau - K_\tau}^{\tau} Z_{ij}(t)\, dt + \int_{\tau - K\, \tau - \delta_{ij}}^{\tau} Z_{ij}(t)\, dt \right] \qquad 3{:}4$$

$$\equiv \int_{\tau - K(\tau)}^{\tau} Z(t)\, dt + \sum_{i=1}^{n} \sum_{j=1}^{m} \delta_{ij}\, Z_{ij}\, (\tau - K_\tau - \epsilon_{ij}), \qquad 3{:}5$$

wherein ϵ is a small unspecified interval of time. Substituting $K_{ij}(\tau) - K_\tau$ for δ_{ij} we have

$$Y_\tau \equiv Y_\tau + \sum_{i=1}^{n} \sum_{j=1}^{m} \left[K_{ij}(\tau) - K_\tau \right]\left[Z_{ij}(\tau - K_\tau - \epsilon_{ij}) \right] \qquad 3{:}6$$

$$K_\tau . \sum_{i=1}^{n} \sum_{j=1}^{m} Z_{ij}(\tau - K_\tau - \epsilon_{ij}) = \sum_{i=1}^{n} \sum_{j=1}^{m} K_{ij}(\tau) Z_{ij}(\tau - K_\tau - \epsilon_{ij}). \qquad 3{:}7$$

Factoring out K we have

$$K_\tau = \frac{\displaystyle\sum_{i=1}^{n} \sum_{j=1}^{m} K_{ij}(\tau) Z_{ij}(\tau - K_\tau - \epsilon_{ij})}{\displaystyle\sum_{i=1}^{n} \sum_{j=1}^{m} Z_{ij}(\tau - K_\tau - \epsilon_{ij})}. \qquad 3{:}8$$

Since the value of ϵ is negligible on the average, we may conclude that

$$K_\tau = \frac{\displaystyle\sum_{i=1}^{n} \sum_{j=1}^{m} K_{ij}\, Z_{ij}\, (\tau - K_\tau)}{\displaystyle\sum_{i=1}^{n} \sum_{j=1}^{m} Z_{ij}\, (\tau - K_\tau)}. \qquad 3{:}9$$

In other words, K is a weighted average of all the individual K_{ij}'s where the weights are the rates of purchase of the given quantum of Y_{ij} at time $\tau - K_\tau$. It is important to note the use of the indefinite article in the last statement, for it reminds us of the fact that K_τ is not the only conceivable average period of turnover of all wealth. It is also important to note that services are assumed to have the same period of turnover as the items of tangible wealth to which they are directly or indirectly applied.

Since we have shown that K_T in formula 3:1 is a national average period of turnover of capital, we may say that the formula expresses the total value of capital at any given time as a function of the total rate of purchases at several times and the average period of turnover of tangible goods. But total purchases at any given moment equal total sales equal total inflow of funds (income) equals total outflow of funds (expenditures) equals total input of goods and services equals total output of goods and services (valued at cost to the buyers). Hence, in the deductions which can be made from formula 3:1 we may call $Z(t)$ by any one of its six names, depending upon which concept is most meaningful in the given circumstances.

The first deduction we wish to make from formula 3:1 is a statement concerning the rate of increase of total capital. We reach this conclusion by differentiation of the formula, viz.

$$\frac{dY}{dt} \equiv [Z(t) - Z(t\text{-}K)] + \frac{dK}{dt} \cdot Z\,(t\text{-}K), \qquad\qquad 3\text{:}10$$

$$\equiv \frac{\partial Y}{\partial Z} \cdot \frac{dZ}{dt} + \frac{\partial Y}{\partial K} \cdot \frac{dK}{dt}. \qquad\qquad 3\text{:}10a$$

This result is a mixed difference-differential equation in which the difference term and the differential term each has an important economic significance. The difference term could be called the gain in purchases or sales (or other things) during the average period of turnover. But the most meaningful nomenclature would seem to be attained by calling the difference term the gain in total income over the period of turnover, while holding turnover constant. For short we choose to label the difference term "the rate of new income," $I\,(t)$, so that

$$I(t) \equiv Z\,(t) - Z\,(t\text{-}K). \qquad\qquad 3\text{:}11$$

The differential term in 3:10 gives the rate of increase of total capital which results from an increase in the period of turnover, *while holding income constant.* The partial derivative $\frac{\partial Y}{\partial K}$ in formula 3:10a has a positive sign, so that when $\frac{dK}{dt}$ is positive the conservation of capital is positive. That is to say, if income remains constant while the period of turnover is increased, there will be an increase in the value of total capital. A convenient name for this differential term would therefore seem to be "the rate of conservation of capital," i.e., the rate of increase in capital which results from making the capital "last longer." Capital is conserved, then, by slowing down its rate of turnover or increasing the period K. We may give this differential term the symbol $\sigma(t)$, and then 3:10 reduces to

$$\frac{dY}{dt} = I(t) + \sigma(t). \qquad 3:12$$

We may write the fundamental equation 3:10 for the individual, as distinguished from society as a whole, by simply hanging the subscript ij on the variables to indicate the value of the $i\,th$ good in the hands of the $j\,th$ trader, viz.

$$\frac{dY_{ij}}{dt} = [Z_{ij}(t) - Z_{ij}(t\text{-}K_{ij})] + \frac{dK_{ij}}{dt} \cdot Z_{ij}(t\text{-}K_{ij}). \qquad 3:13$$

Despite the symmetry of formula 3:13 with respect to formula 3:10, the formula for the individual does not quite have a meaning that is equivalent to the meaning of the aggregate formula. This is because $Z_{ij}(t)$ is not equal to *both* the rate of purchase of capital by the individual and his rate of receipt of (gross) income. Its meaning must be confined to rate of purchase of capital. Hence, in the simplified version of 3:13

$$\frac{dY_{ij}}{dt} = I_{ij}(t) + \sigma_{ij}(t), \qquad 3:14$$

the difference term, I, cannot be called the new income of the individual but rather should be called his "new purchases." The individual's differential term $\frac{dK_{ij}}{dt} Z_{ij}(t - K_{ij})$ or $\sigma(t)_{ij}$ may fairly be called his rate of conservation of capital of the $i\,th$ type.

By simple definition

$$\Sigma \frac{dY_{ij}}{dt} = \frac{dY}{dt} = [Z(t) - Z(t - K)] + \frac{dK}{dt} \cdot Z(t - K), \qquad 3:15$$

and so the individual formulae for rate of increase of the value of a given kind of good in the hand of a given trader may be summed throughout the economy. We may also say that $\Sigma Z_{ij}(t) = Z(t)$ while $\Sigma Z_{ij}(t\text{-}K_{ij}) = Z(t\text{-}K)$; that is to say, there exists some average value of the K_{ij}'s which makes this last equation true. One may deduce intuitively that this average value of the K_{ij}'s is about the same as the K we were dealing with in formula 3:10. In this case it follows that the sum of the individual rates of conservation is equal to the national rate of conservation, $\sigma(t)$, as defined by formula 3:10.

In order to convert formula 3:10 into one which may be compared with the stochastic data, it is necessary to integrate the formula over a period of time equal to the duration for which the national data are accumulated in the available research materials. If ϵ is the period of accumulation for the economy as a whole, we have the following:

$$\int_{\tau-\epsilon}^{\tau} \frac{dY}{dt}\, dt = \int_{\tau-\epsilon}^{\tau} [Z(t) - Z(t-K)]\, dt + \int_{\tau-\epsilon}^{\tau} \frac{dK}{dt} \cdot Z(t-K)\, dt. \qquad 3:16$$

In formula 3:16 all integrals are expressed in dollars rather than in dollars per period of time as is the case for the integrand expression. In this formula, τ is the moment of time at the end of the accounting period. We may abbreviate formula 3:16 to read

$$\Delta Y(\tau) = I(\tau) + \sigma(\tau), \qquad 3:17$$

wherein $\Delta Y(\tau)$ is the increase of capital during the accounting period, $I(\tau)$ is the accumulated new income during the period, and $\sigma(\tau)$ is the accumulated conservation of capital. Formula 3:17 is distinguished from 3:12 by the use of τ instead of t to indicate that reference is made not to instantaneous rates but rather to dollar amounts accumulated for the accounting (or statistical) period.

Earlier in the chapter we wrote the total value of capital at any given time as a function of Z and K: that is, $Y(t) = f[Z(t), K(t)]$. By the theory of inverse functions we know that the value of Z at any given time may be written as a function of Y and K, viz., $Z = F(Y, K)$. Differentiation of this inverse function leads to this result:

$$\frac{dZ}{dt} = \frac{\partial F}{\partial Y} \cdot \frac{dY}{dt} + \frac{\partial F}{\partial K} \cdot \frac{dK}{dt} \qquad 3:18$$

Substituting 3:18 in formula 3:10a, we have

$$\frac{dY}{dt} = \left[\frac{\partial f}{\partial Z} \cdot \frac{\partial F}{\partial Y} \cdot \frac{dY}{dt} + \frac{\partial f}{\partial Z} \cdot \frac{\partial F}{\partial K} \cdot \frac{dK}{dt} \right] + \frac{\partial f}{\partial K} \cdot \frac{dK}{dt} \qquad 3:19$$

where the bracket term is the rate of new income. Furthermore we know by the theory of inverse functions that

$$\frac{\partial f}{\partial Z} \cdot \frac{\partial F}{\partial Y} \equiv 1.00 \qquad 3:20$$

Hence, by substitution of 3:20 in 3:19 we have

$$\frac{dY}{dt} \equiv \frac{dY}{dt} + \frac{\partial f}{\partial Z} \cdot \frac{\partial F}{\partial K} \cdot \frac{dK}{dt} + \frac{\partial f}{\partial K} \cdot \frac{dK}{dt}. \qquad 3:21$$

And as a result

$$\frac{\partial f}{\partial Z} \cdot \frac{\partial F}{\partial K} \cdot \frac{dK}{dt} = -\frac{\partial f}{\partial K} \cdot \frac{dK}{dt}. \qquad 3:22$$

Since the term on the right has been labelled the rate of conservation of capital, the term on the left is entitled to be called "the rate of anti-conservation of capital," because it is equal to the rate of conservation with the sign reversed. Since $\frac{\partial f}{\partial K}$ is always positive, the sign of conservation is always the same as the sign of dK; that is to say, there is positive conservation in the economy as a whole whenever the average period of turnover of capital is increasing. But the sign of $\frac{\partial f}{\partial Z}$ is always positive, while the sign of $\frac{\partial F}{\partial K}$ is always negative. It is this negative sign of $\frac{\partial F}{\partial K}$ that causes the left-hand side of 3:22 to be negative when the right-hand side is positive.

The rate of new investment, valued at cost to the investor, is equal by definition to the rate of increase of capital valued at cost, because a given increment of capital can only turn over once during the period of its "newness." Hence, if $\gamma(t)$ is the rate of new investment—or the rate of investment for short—we have the identity

$$\frac{dY}{dt} \equiv \gamma(t). \qquad 3:23$$

By substitution of 3:20, 3:22, and 3:23 in 3:19 we reach the conclusion that

$$\frac{dY}{dt} = [\gamma(t) - \sigma(t)] + \sigma(t) \qquad 3:24$$

because $\frac{\partial f}{\partial K} \frac{dK}{dt}$, the rate of conservation of capital, has been designated as $\sigma(t)$ for short.

Formula 3:24 tells us that, for the economy as a whole, the rate of increase (decrease) of total capital is equal to the rate of investment plus the rate of anti-conservation of capital plus the rate of conservation of capital. Moreover,

$$\sigma(t) = \frac{\partial f}{\partial K} \cdot \frac{dK}{dt} = \frac{dK}{dt} \cdot Z(t-K) \qquad 3:25$$

and hence, by reference to formula 3:15 above, we see that the bracket term in 3:24 is equal to the bracket term in 3:15. This means that the bracket term in 3:24 is the rate of new income.

Thus we perceive that there is concealed in the new income of the whole economy a term equal to the anti-conservation of capital. Thus, also, it is impossible in an exchange economy for the traders as a whole to increase their total capital by conserving their capital. The increase which one trader gains by conserving his capital is exactly offset by a loss of input received by another trader, and this loss of input is translated into a reduction of his capital. Thus for the whole economy, the effect of the conservation of capital on the money value of total capital is exactly neutral. But the effect of the conservation of capital on the income of society is rather devastating.

TABLE 2

NEW INCOME IN THE UNITED STATES COMPARED WITH THE CONSERVATION OF CAPITAL (BILLIONS OF DOLLARS)

Year	Rate of New Income	Rate of Conservation of Capital	Year	Rate of New Income	Rate of Conservation of Capital
1922	- 30.3	+17.63	1940	+53.02	- 15.39
1923	+58.90	- 25.25	1941	+141.93	- 83.27
1924	+44.77	- 15.65	1942	+186.32	- 128.65
1925	+41.88	- 9.12	1943	+216.54	- 155.38
1926	+44.52	- 9.15	1944	+174.04	- 106.66
1927	+19.34	+14.09	1945	+90.90	- 11.62
1928	+27.01	+ 7.59	1946	+95.17	- 12.99
1929	+34.09	+ 5.93	1947	+188.22	- 100.41
1930	- 52.98	+98.77	1948	+178.76	- 75.73
1931	- 125.30	+158.88	1949	+54.87	+43.98
1932	- 183.03	+202.11	1950	+97.19	+15.13
1933	- 194.15	+126.22	1951	+229.37	- 103.08
1934	- 118.90	+126.22	1952	+171.32	- 45.73
1935	- 32.06	+49.08	1953	+106.05	+30.91
1936	+66.82	- 33.66	1954	+37.88	+86.04
1937	+118.67	- 84.86	1955	+118.24	+14.84
1938	+53.27	- 25.94	1956	+205.58	- 70.37
1939	+65.35	- 25.45			

This is true because in the formula for the rate of new income of society, namely

$$I(t) = \gamma(t) - \sigma(t), \qquad 3:26$$

there is usually no positive element large enough to offset the reduction caused by the anti-conservation term. To be sure, there is in 3:26 the investment term $\gamma(t)$ which might conceivably be positive

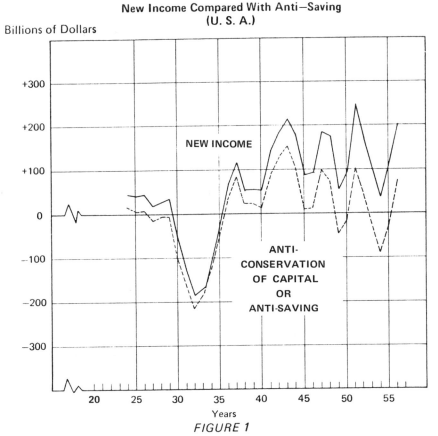

FIGURE 1

when the conservation of capital is positive, and in that case $\gamma(t)$ might buffer the negative effect of conservation on new income. However, the trouble with this line of argument is that, for psychological reasons, when people are conserving their use of existing capital, they are not likely to be investing in new capital. Thus investment tends to be negative when conservation is positive. In practice we tend to get a double-barreled reduction of income when conservation is positive; that is, a reduction due to negative investment as well as a much larger reduction due to the conservation of capital. We say much larger because, in the period of 36 years for which we have examined the data, we have found the amplitude of the fluctuations of σ is several times as large as the amplitude of the fluctuations of γ.

Hence it follows that when the conservation of capital is positively valued, the economy is almost invariably undergoing a recession. In other words, a graph of new income without correction for trend will give a good picture of the direction of movement of total business. The truth of this statement may be seen by inspecting Figure I, in which we have drawn a curve representing new income in the United States, without correction for trend, for a period of 36 years, as well as a curve showing the rate of anti-conservation of capital, also without correction for trend.

It will be noted that there is an almost perfect correlation between the directions of movement of the two curves in the chart. Furthermore, there is a startling dip in the new income data to indicate the great depression of the thirties, as well as minor dips in response to the recessions of 1937, 1945, 1949, and 1954. The correlation coefficient between new income and anti-conservation is in the low nineties. This high correlation is not a spurious one which might result from a similarity of long-term trends, because there is no detectable trend at all in the data for anti-conservation for the period of 36 years. The dissimilarity of trend causes the correlation coefficient $r_{I\sigma}$ to be spuriously low rather than high.

It is clear that formula 3:19 applies to the individual as well as to society. Thus we have, by symmetry,

$$\frac{dY_i}{dt} = \left[\frac{\partial f_i}{\partial Z_i} \cdot \frac{\partial F_i}{\partial Y_i} \cdot \frac{dY_i}{dt} + \frac{\partial f_i}{\partial Z_i} \cdot \frac{\partial F_i}{\partial K_i} \cdot \frac{dK_i}{dt} \right] + \frac{\partial f_i}{\partial K_i} \cdot \frac{dK_i}{dt} \cdot \qquad 3:27$$

This shows that there is a negative term in the individual's new input equal to the positive conservation of capital achieved by the individual. However, the individual may be able to hold his input constant while decreasing his output by conserving capital. In the whole economy, on the other hand, one man's output (at cost) is another man's input (abstracting from price inflation or deflation). If a given individual decreases his output, another trader (or traders) must have his (or their) input decreased accordingly. Barring price inflation or deflation, we might have the following respective values for the terms in formula 3:27

$$+ 1.00 = [+ 1 - 1/3 \times 3] + 1/3 \times 3 = +1.00. \qquad 3:28$$

The individual's anti-conservation is equal to his conservation, but just the same he is able to increase his capital by +1, the amount of his conservation, because we have assumed that he is able to hold his input constant, so that the solution to

$$\frac{dY_i}{dt} = Z_i(t) - Z_i(t\text{-}K_i) + \frac{dK_i}{dt} Z_i(t\text{-}K_i) \qquad 3:29$$

might read this way

$$+ 1 = [+1 -1] + 1/3 \times 3 = + 1. \qquad 3:30$$

This solution might imply the following reaction in the rest of the economy, assuming that no other change is initiated in the rest of society:

$$- 1 = [-1 +0] - 0 = - 1 \qquad 3:31$$

The effect of conservation by one trader on the whole economy is given by adding 3:30 and 3:31, *viz.*

$$0 = 0 + [-1] +1/3 \times 3 = 0. \qquad 3:32$$

Thus it follows that, with a stable price level, society cannot increase the value of its tangible capital by the conservation of existing capital. A modicum of inflation is perhaps necessary to offset the depressing effect of a conservation of goods on the money value of the total income of society. Inevitably the primary problem of state regulation of business is the problem of inflation: that is, the problem of how best to provide a modicum of inflation by credit and fiscal policy, while preventing a surfeit of inflation with all of its demoralizing consequences. The egregious difference between the effect of conservation upon the individual and upon the whole economy is certainly a leading paradox of economic theory. And attempts to resolve this paradox by a resort to "Crusoe" economics (e.g., simplistic classical theory) are worthless or worse.

A formula for the total rate of expense of the whole economy can be produced by manipulation of formula 3:10 above. The rate of expense is an important factor in total business fluctuations. By common sense the rate of increase of capital is equal to the rate of sales minus the rate of expense. If $E(t)$ is the total rate of expense, we have by definition

$$E(t) = Z(t) - \gamma(t). \qquad 3{:}33$$

It will be remembered that $\gamma(t)$, the rate of new investment, is equal to the rate of increase of capital for society as a whole. The substitution of formula 3:10 in 3:33 yields this statement of the value of the total rate of expense:

$$E(t) = Z(t) - \left\{ [Z(t) - Z(t\text{-}K)] + \frac{dK}{dt} \cdot Z(t\text{-}K) \right\} \qquad 3{:}34$$

$$= Z(t\text{-}K) - \frac{dK}{dt} \cdot Z(t\text{-}K). \qquad 3{:}35$$

Thus we come to perceive that the total rate of expense for society as a whole at time t is equal to the total rate of sales at time t - K minus the rate of conservation of capital at time t. If the rate of conservation of capital at a given time is zero, then the total rate of expense at that time is simply the total rate of sales (or purchases) at an earlier time. In other words, under the stated conditions and under the rule of first in, first out, today's output (i.e., expense) is quite simply the value of the tangible goods (and the services attached to them) that were purchased at an earlier time. But, for the whole economy, total sales are equal to total purchases, and so expense at present is equal to total sales at an earlier time, if there is no conservation of capital, and no inflation.

On the other hand, if the conservation of capital is positive at a given time, it means that not all of the goods purchased at time t - K will pass out into the flow of expenses due to the fact that the period of turnover of goods is being lengthened. The effect of the conservation of capital is to reduce the rate of expense by the rate given by $\frac{dK}{dt} \cdot Z(t$ - $K)$, as is shown by formula 3:35.

In the special case of zero conservation, the total rate of output of all traders is equal to the rate at which they were "inputting" tangible goods and services K years back in ordered time. This checks with common sense under the assumed condition that the average period of turnover of all wealth, K, be kept constant. If everything now being sold has been held by the present sellers for K years, and K is not changing, then what is being sold at the present moment was bought K years ago, and everything which was purchased exactly K years ago is being sold at the present moment.

This would be unquestionably true with regard to circulating capital, such as raw materials, which materials are bought at one date and sold, subject to a bill of sale specifying the same units of mass (as modified perhaps by manufacture), K years later. It is less obvious, perhaps, but it is nevertheless mathematically true that formula 3:35 also applies to "fixed" capital if we consider that such capital is "sold" by the owner as it is charged to depreciation, and if we assume that the life histories of fixed assets are averaged appropriately into the evaluation of K for the economy as a whole.

We have defined the instantaneous rate of new income as $I(t)$ where

$$I(t) = Z(t) - Z(t - K). \qquad 3:36$$

This function may also be expressed by the following:

$$I(t) = \int_{t-K}^{t} \frac{dZ}{dt} \cdot dt \qquad 3:37$$

Thus the dimension of the rate of increase of rate of income, $\frac{dZ}{dt}$, is dollars per period of time per period of time. But the dimension of $I(t)$, the rate of *new* income is dollars per period of time, because the rate of increase of income has to be integrated over the period K in order to become the rate of new income. The integration process accomplishes two things: (1) it converts the dimension of the integrand function to a variable with a time dimension equal to that of the rate of new investment and (2) it gives a numerical value to the concept which makes it equal to the rate of new investment when there is no conservation of capital.

The integrating process therefore performs the work of what may be called a dimensional operator. This may be seen from an alternative expression for the rate of new income, namely:

$$I(t) = \frac{\partial f}{\partial Z} \cdot \frac{dZ}{dt}, \qquad 3:38$$

wherein $Y = f(Z, K)$. The partial derivative $\dfrac{\partial f}{\partial Z}$ in this expression does the necessary work of integration which was performed in formula 3:37 and it serves the same purpose of changing the dimension and numerical value of $\dfrac{dZ}{dt}$ in order to make it comparable with the rate of new income. $\dfrac{\partial f}{\partial Z}$ is therefore correctly called a dimensional operator in the theory of business fluctuations.

In order to get the value of new income received in an accounting period, ϵ, the rate of new income must be integrated over such an accounting period. If $I(\tau)$ is the new income for the period of time in question,

$$I(\tau) \equiv \int_{T-\epsilon}^{T} \int_{t-K}^{t} \frac{dZ}{dt} \cdot dt\, dt. \qquad 3:39$$

The dimension of $I(\tau)$ is plain dollars, as distinguished from the dimension of $I(t)$ which is dollars per period of time. For the purpose of statistical verification, formula 3:39 may be put in this way:

$$I(\tau) \equiv \int_{T-\epsilon}^{T} [Z(t) - Z(t\text{-}K)]\, dt. \qquad 3:40$$

$$\doteq \int_{T-\epsilon}^{T} Z(t)dt - \int_{T-K-\epsilon}^{T-K} Z(t)dt, \qquad 3:41$$

$$\doteq Z(\tau) - Z(\tau\text{-}K), \qquad 3:42$$

which tells us that the new income received in the accounting period ending at time $t = \tau$ is approximately equal to the total income received in that period less the total income received in an accounting period which ended K years earlier. Thus the correct measurement of new income requires the use of two intervals of integration, namely, a constant one equal to the length of the accounting period and a variable interval equal to K, the average period of turnover of tangible goods.[1]

---

[1] Rate of change of accumulated income for some arbitrary and fixed interval of time is, to be sure, a variable with only a single time dimension (like the rate of change of total capital) but recognition of this fact does not alter in any way the fundamental difficulty which must be resolved. To employ one year as the interval of integration is to make the wholly unwarranted assumptions that (1) the proper interval of accumulation for the purpose at hand is a constant and (2) whatever fixed interval comes most readily to mind is the proper one to use in estimating the rate of new income.

If one compared the yearly rate of change of income accumulated by years, this would

Some writers have treated the measurement of new income as if *both* intervals of integration were equal to the accounting period, which they generally take to be a year. Thus they come up with a measurement of new income which is mathematically stated as follows:

$$I'(\tau) \doteqdot \int_{\tau-\epsilon}^{\tau} Z(t)dt - \int_{\tau-2\epsilon}^{\tau-\epsilon} Z(t)dt, \qquad 3{:}43$$

where I' is an incorrect measurement of I. The true value of new income for this year is not the total income of this year minus the total income of last year, as stated by formula 3:43. In order for that to be true, the average period of turnover of goods would have to be equal to one year, which it has never been, or at least has not been in modern times.

This notion of a dimensional operator is to be distinguished from a mere *multiplier*. A multiplier is a fairly constant coefficient having no dimension; that is, it is a "pure" number which appears in an equation involving economic variables. It does not change the dimension of any variable but serves merely to equate those variables which already have the same dimension.

Going back to formula 3:19 we see the existence of dimensional operators on the right-hand side. Consider the expression $\dfrac{\partial f}{\partial Z} \dfrac{\partial F}{\partial Y} \dfrac{dY}{dt}$, which gives the rate of new investment, $\gamma(t)$. On the one hand, the rate of new investment valued at cost may be defined as the rate of purchase of rate of increment of capital. By this definition $\gamma(t)$ is defined as

$$\gamma(t) = \frac{\partial F}{\partial Y} \cdot \frac{dY}{dt}. \qquad 3{:}44$$

This is true because the partial derivative $\dfrac{\partial F}{\partial Y}$ gives the average rate of turnover of new capital, whereas the rate of new capital formation

---

involve making the assumption, without any logical support, that "old income" is always properly taken to mean last year's income, year in and year out, without regard to business fluctuations. Any empirical relationship which might be observed over a number of years between increase of capital and "new" income so conceived would be more or less coincidental and would demonstrate once more the unreliability of statistical correlations between time series which are supported only by an empirical similarity of behavior.

If K were a constant equal to (say) two years, the use of ϵ equal to one year as the interval of integration to measure new income would produce, if the rate of change of rate of income were likewise constant, an evaluation of new income for the year ending at time $t = \tau$ which would show only half the true value.

is given by the total derivative $\frac{dY}{dt}$. Thus formula 3:44 gives the number of times new capital is being bought and sold multiplied by the rate at which new capital is coming on the market. The dimension of $\frac{\partial F}{\partial Y}$ is times per period of time and the dimension of $\frac{dY}{dt}$ is dollars per period of time. Hence, the dimension of $\gamma(t)$ as defined by formula 3:44 is dollars per period of time per period of time. However, the common sense evaluation of rate of new investment (valued at cost) is simply the rate at which total capital (valued at cost) is increasing. So conceived, the rate of new investment has only one time dimension; that is, it has the dimension of dollars per period of time.

Hence, we have two definitions of the rate of new investment, *viz.*

$$\gamma(t) = \frac{\partial F}{\partial Y} \cdot \frac{dY}{dt}, \qquad\qquad 3:45$$

and

$$\gamma(t) = \frac{dY}{dt}. \qquad\qquad 3:46$$

Plainly a dimensional operator is needed in order to reconcile the two concepts of rate of new investment, one of which has a double time dimension (like the rate of increase of new income) and the other a single time dimension. The correct dimensional operator must also reconcile the numerical values of 3:44 and 3:46. Reference to formula 3:19 above will show that the necessary dimensional operator is given by the partial derivative $\frac{\partial f}{\partial Z}$. This partial derivative has the dimension of period of time, and it is the reciprocal of $\frac{\partial F}{\partial Y}$ in 3:45. This dimensional operator, when multiplied by the right-hand side of 3:45 will bring about the equality of the two definitions of rate of new investment, *viz.*

$$\gamma(t) = \frac{\partial f}{\partial Z} \cdot \frac{\partial F}{\partial Y} \cdot \frac{dY}{dt} = \frac{dY}{dt}. \qquad\qquad 3:47$$

The reconciliation causes both formulations of rate of new investment to be of the dimension dollars per period of time, and the numerical values are likewise the same.

Some readers might suspect that our basic assumption of "first in, first out" in the order of alienation of capital is unrealistic in view of the many tax dodges which invite a departure from this rule in accounting procedure. The answer is that such departures are restricted by the physical compulsion of a realistic accountancy. As a matter of necessity the older generators in a power plant have to be retired before the newer ones in the usual case, the decayed ties in a railroad roadbed have to be replaced before the newer ones, and the older buildings are usually torn down before the more modern structures. In further rebuttal of criticism, we are inclined to say that "the proof of the pudding is in the eating." Give us leave to make our basic assumption and let us proceed to derive fundamental relationships which must exist between business aggregates on the basis of that assumption. Then if statistical verification yields a high degree of agreement between fact and theory, it would seem to follow that the assumption made in theory is realistic. Figure I of this chapter has already shown to a remarkable degree the basic relationship between two important factors in business fluctuations which was predicted in theory.[2]

---

[2]The reason all the experimental data in this work end in 1956 or 1957 is not the sloth of the authors nor is it any craven fear that later numbers would not continue to verify our theory. The Federal Reserve abruptly ceased publication of the raw data we need in 1957. They spent about $7 million in gathering the raw data of their Tableaux Economiques. It is beyond the physical or financial means of the authors to provide such costly material. We have our computerized program for our model in our files and we would be glad to feed additional data into this program whenever it is made available. There is not the slightest doubt that our relationships are inviolable by time under a pecuniary, profit motivated society.

A letter to the Federal Reserve Board imploring them to resume publication of the data we need elicited the inane reply that such data can be *inferred* from other series still published by the Board. This statement simply is not true.

Chapter 4

THE CONCEPT OF SAVINGS OF
SOCIETY AS A WHOLE

Classical economic thought defined the value of total savings as the difference between total personal income and total expenditures for consumer goods. New investment was taken to be limited by and equal to the value of total savings. Savers were said to tighten their belts in order to make savings deposits or otherwise make funds available at financial institutions for the purchase of new capital goods by borrowers. The excess of income over expenditures implied a postponement of consumption by the savers. The temporary self-sacrifice or abstinence coincident with saving had to be rewarded by the payment of interest on the savings, if the total volume of savings per period were to be made equal to the quantity demanded. Savers were considered to be entitled to such a reward for their self-denial and waiting in making available the huge funds required by investors to promote the progress of the economy.

In real terms, this analysis made a great deal of sense. Society's resources (land, labor, and capital) are given at any particular point in time. The borrowers' objective in borrowing is to obtain command or control of a larger proportion of society's resources than they could have obtained on their own power. The attainment of this objective will be impossible, however, unless other people (the savers) relinquish at least temporarily command or control over a portion of the resources which they could have used for their own purposes by spending their entire incomes. Thus, control of a part of society's real resources is transferred from savers to borrowers, and savers receive interest for accepting future use of such resources in the place of present use.

The analysis does not make nearly so much sense in monetary

49

terms. The rationale of the relationship between savings and investment implies that savings in the bank (or other financial institution)
may be transferred by the bank from the savers' accounts to those of
the borrowers or investors. But this kind of transfer is prohibited by
laws against embezzlement and wrongful conversion. The demand
deposit of A is, physically speaking, merely a figure printed on a
computer tape. When the individual transfers funds from his drawing
account to a savings account, the bank is empowered to transfer
this figure from one tape to another, with A's name still attached
to it. If the B corporation wants funds to enlarge its plant and seeks
the funds at A's bank, the bank cannot legally transfer the printed
figure aforementioned from A's place on the tape to B's place on
the tape. Thus the monetary savings of one party cannot be invested
by another party merely because a bank has received a savings
deposit.

Why then do banks pay interest on savings deposits if they cannot
make productive use of them? The answer lies in the relationship
of an individual bank to the whole banking system. When A transfers
his funds from a demand deposit to a savings account he serves
notice on the bank, in effect, that he does not intend to make use of
the funds in the near future. That is to say, the bank can feel confident that it will not suffer the possible embarrassment of having to
pay out the funds to another bank where the funds have turned up
as a result of their being spent by A. The demand deposit is in
effect a printed number on a tape which indicates a promise or
obligation of A's bank to pay out this number of dollars on demand
by $A,$ or by other parties to whom A has transferred his rights. If
the other parties, in turn, transfer these rights to another bank, the
second bank may demand that the first bank pay to it an equivalent
of the reserve money held by the first bank.

This transfer of reserve funds would weaken the ability of the
first bank to *create* new funds in the form of demand deposits to be
borrowed by the investing B corporation. The transfer of funds by
A to the savings account tape tends to increase the confidence of A's
bank in creating funds for investment by the B corporation. And
this is the only sense in which savings deposits can be used to increase
the funds available for investment.

As we intend to show in a later chapter, the total rate of new
investment in the economy is equal to the rate of expenditure of

funds newly created to finance new investment. Since this is true, the rate of saving by society as a whole, as discussed above, cannot directly add to new investment, for the effect of saving on total investment must be a second-order effect resulting from psychological considerations. Furthermore, we shall show that, while an individual's saving may stimulate the creation of funds for investment by a single bank by making the banker more confident, the effect of saving by the whole economy on the total creation of fresh funds is usually depressing rather than stimulating.

The reason is that total saving, when properly defined, is positively correlated with the rate of conservation of capital, and the latter rate is negatively correlated with new income, as we have shown. When total income is going down, bankers feel apprehensive rather than confident. Prospective investors are also fearful, and the operation of the whole machinery for the creation of investment funds (including other creators than banks) is slowed.

From the financial viewpoint, the newly created funds used to invest in new capital cannot have been withdrawn from the national income stream because they are committed to the income stream for the first time when they are used to buy new capital, almost at the moment of their creation. But what about the situation at the date of maturity of the new credit instruments (new funds) which are used to finance new investment? Will not the payment and retirement of these obligations by debtors constitute or require saving in the usual sense of the word in the year of maturity? Why, not at all. In the year of retirement of the formerly "new" funds, the rate of investment in new capital goods will once again equal the rate of expenditure of funds created in the newly "new" year for such purpose. That is to say, the investment of the newly "new" period will once again be financed largely with "new" funds. This means, of course, that the old new funds will be refunded, if not by the original debtors then by other debtors who furnish the original debtors, or their successors, with the funds for refunding, directly or indirectly.

If the funds for refunding are not made available, the lack will cause a decline in the value of total funds, and this will mean an increase in the rate of saving, as properly defined, by virtue of the tendency of new income to decline as a result of the disinvestment. This, in turn, will produce a depression in total income; i.e., a recession in general business or, if the disinvestment is allowed to continue, a severe depression, as in the case of 1929-1933.

Let $M_{ij}(\tau)$ represent the amount of the i th description of positively-valued funds held by the j_{th} individual at time τ. Let S_{ij} be the value of such funds being received at time t by the j_{th} individual. Then we may define the term β_{ij} by the following equation:

$$M_{ij}(\tau) \equiv \int_{\tau-\beta_{ij}}^{\tau} S_{ij}(t)dt. \qquad 4:1$$

This equation defines β_{ij} as the interval of time over which past receipts of M_{ij} have to be accumulated in order to arrive at a numerical result equal to the value of this kind of funds being held by the j th trader at time $t = \tau$. The individual trader may not have a continuous rate of receipt of funds, as is implied by the function $S_{ij}(t)$. In his case, then, we have in mind a continuous function which approximates the discontinuous one of reality.

Since the supply of a given fund in the hands of a given trader is more or less fungible, we do not have any way to measure precisely the historical period of turnover of the quantum M_{ij}. However, if we assume in general that the alienation of any given type of fund has proceeded according to the principle of "first in, first out," then it can be shown by a physical experiment that β_{ij} is the historical period of turnover of the i th type of funds in the hands of the j th trader.

Certainly the said funds do have a period of turnover. And we cannot measure this period of turnover by the formula S_{ij}/M_{ij} because for the individual S_{ij} is his rate of receipt of funds and not his rate of expenditure thereof, whereas the period of turnover is the duration of time between receipt and expenditure by the same individual. It is not necessary to assume explicitly that each trader *thinks* he is alienating funds according to the principle of "first in, first out." If we assume that, in general, funds are being alienated according to this systematic scheme, important conclusions can be drawn with respect to the savings of the economy as a whole, which conclusions can be subjected to the test of statistical verification.

Let $M(\tau)$ be the total supply of positively-valued funds at time $t = \tau$, while $S(t)$ is the rate of receipt of the said funds by all traders at time t. Then we may define the function $\beta(\tau)$ by the formula

$$M(\tau) \equiv \int_{\tau-\beta}^{\tau} S(t)dt. \qquad 4:2$$

Formula 4:2 is symmetrical with respect to formula 3:1 just as the family of formulas 4:1 are symmetrical with respect to the formulas 3:2. It follows that the mathematical relationship of β to the various β_{ij} is the same as that of K with respect to the various K_{ij}. This means that the variable β may be regarded as a weighted average period of turnover of funds just as K may be regarded as a weighted average period of turnover of goods.

Therefore, differentiation of formula 4:2 produces the interesting result that, since $M = f(S, \beta)$, when the values are taken at various stated intervals:

$$dM = \frac{\partial M}{\partial S}\, dS + \frac{\partial M}{\partial \beta}\, d\beta, \qquad 4:3$$

and

$$\frac{dM}{dt} \equiv [S(t) - S(t\text{-}\beta)] + \frac{d\beta}{dt} S(t\text{-}\beta). \qquad 4:4$$

This mixed difference and differential equation states that the rate of increase of total (positively-valued) funds is equal to the rate of new receipts (the difference or bracket term) plus the differential term, $\frac{d\beta}{dt} \cdot S(t-\beta)$. If the differential term should happen to be zero, the rate of increase of funds at any given time would be given quite simply as the difference between the rate of receipts of funds at time t and the rate of receipts of funds at an earlier time, $t - \beta$. Moreover, for the economy as a whole, the rate of expenditure equals the rate of receipt of funds: so the bracket term tells us that, for society as a whole, the rate of receipt of new funds is equal to the present rate of *expenditure* minus the rate of expenditure at an earlier time, if the differential term in 4:4 is zero.

On the other hand, if the new receipts are zero, the rate of increase of funds is equal to the effect produced by changing the average period of turnover, β. If β is increasing, it will *tend* to increase the supply of funds, M. When β is increasing it means that people are postponing their expenditures, and this will *tend* to make the output of funds less than it would otherwise be, thereby *tending* to increase the supply of funds. In other words, the differential term in formula 4:4 gives the increase in funds brought about by the conservation of funds (if other things remain the same). It is therefore rightfully regarded as the rate of saving by society as a whole, because to conserve funds is to postpone their expenditure. If $\zeta(t)$ represents the value of saving by society as a whole, we have then defined this important variable by the formula

$$\zeta(t) = \frac{d\beta}{dt} \cdot S(t-\beta). \qquad\qquad 4:5$$

This formula tells us that the rate of saving in the whole economy is equal to the rate of increase in the period of turnover of funds multiplied by the rate of receipt of funds at time $t - \beta$. The precise mathematical formula for saving must be one which evaluates the combined economic effect of (1) an act of a certain pecuniary nature and (2) the reaction resulting therefrom on the total supply of funds. The rate of saving for society as a whole is, if you please, that part of the increase in the supply of funds which would be achieved by the postponement of the expenditure of funds, other things remaining the same. This postponement of expenditure may or may not be achieved by the transfer of funds from a category which is turning over at a certain rate to a category which is rotating more slowly in the exchange of goods and services.

The transfer of funds from a bank account payable on demand to a savings account is universally thought of as an act of saving by the person (real or corporate) who does such a thing. Another example would be the utilization of funds in a demand account for the purchase of an outstanding government bond. In both of these cases the average rate of turnover of the saver's funds has presumably been lowered by the transaction. Conversely, the average *period* of turnover of his funds has been increased. The essential nature of *either* transaction in connection with the evaluation of saving is found precisely in the fact that the velocity of a certain quantum of funds has been reduced, for obviously nothing has happened to the total supply of funds, either of the saver or of the whole of society, by virtue of the saving transaction. And the total expenditure of funds for goods and services will be affected only through a change in the average rate of turnover of funds therefor. If their rate of turnover, or velocity, has been lowered by a given transfer, there has been positive saving; if the velocity has been raised, there has been negative saving.

The famous "man-in-the-street" does not think he has saved anything unless he has engineered a transfer of categories, as above. However, the economist cannot afford to agree with him, because clear thinking requires the scientist to perceive and recognize the fact that the impact which a transfer of funds would have upon general business fluctuations can be achieved without any transfer of funds.

If a similar effect can be achieved in other ways than by transfer of funds, the scientific definition of saving must be broad enough to include similar impacts. The scientist must recognize that a reduction in the velocity of certain funds can be brought about by an individual if he merely allows his funds in a demand account to become more nearly inert. In the correct appraisal of the rate of saving by society as a whole, *all* reductions in the velocity of funds must be accounted for, including those which do not include a transfer of funds, even if the average individual does not recognize the latter as savings.

The average individual thinks of his savings as being exactly equal to the amount of funds which he transfers to a slowly rotating (or non-rotating) category in a given period. The economist cannot agree with this conclusion because it is essential to recognize that the economic impact of saving is a compound function of the value of funds involved and the change in their rate of turnover (or period of turnover) in exchange for goods and services. From the point of view of effective communication it is unfortunate that there should need to be this parting of the ways between the economic scientist and the general public with respect to such important matters. However, precision of thought and analytical usefulness are more important criteria in the definition of concepts than is agreement with popular usage.

The ordinary person would be more nearly correct in his thinking if the funds which he transfers to (say) a savings account were destined to remain in that category *forever*. But this is not true. Sooner or later the funds will be taken out of the savings account and will be spent for goods and services by the individual who "saved" them or by his heirs and assigns or executors. Thus one must not leave duration of time out of account in the evaluation of the rate of saving. The average rate of turnover (or the average period of turnover) takes the duration of time into account, and the rate of change of this average rate of turnover (or period of turnover, obversely) must be applied to the total funds in existence in order to make a correct beginning in the evaluation of the rate of saving. When funds are conserved, their average period of turnover is increased and the value of total saving is given by the formula

$$\zeta(t) = \frac{d\beta}{dt} \cdot S(t\text{-}\beta).$$

4:5

When there is positive saving the sign of the derivative will be positive, as well as the sign of the whole expression, because the value of S is always positive by definition.

Alternatively, when the velocity of funds is increased, the period of turnover is decreased and there will be a negative saving in the whole economy. This negative saving we elect to call *anti-saving*, and it is evaluated by the second term in the bracketed expression for new receipts in formula 4:8. That is, $\rho(t)$, the rate of anti-saving, is given by the following:

$$\rho(t) = \frac{\partial M}{\partial S} \cdot \frac{\partial F}{\partial \beta} \cdot \frac{d\beta}{dt} = -\zeta(t), \qquad\qquad 4:6$$

where it will be remembered that $\frac{d\beta}{dt}$ is the rate of change of the *period* of turnover of funds. A positive $\frac{d\beta}{dt}$ causes a positive rate of saving, as shown by formula 4:5. But the sign of the first partial derivative in 4:6 is positive, whereas the sign of the second partial derivative is negative. Hence the whole expression for ρ will have the opposite sign of $\frac{d\beta}{dt}$ and will be negative when the rate of saving is positive.

Positive saving is therefore concealed as a negative factor in the expression for rate of new receipts. This negative term, or anti-saving, is of course numerically equal to the rate of saving. Hence, as we have said before, a positive saving cannot contribute to an actual increase in the total supply of funds, nor can a negative saving detract therefrom. Positive saving would increase the supply of funds if other things, such as the rate of receipt of funds, could remain constant in the face of positive saving. But it cannot remain constant on account of the anti-saving which is generated by the saving.

By the theorem of inverse functions we know that, if $M = f(S, \beta)$, then $S = F(M, \beta)$, and differentiation of the second expression yields this result:

$$\frac{dS}{dt} = \frac{\partial F}{\partial M} \cdot \frac{dM}{dt} + \frac{\partial F}{\partial \beta} \cdot \frac{d\beta}{dt}. \qquad\qquad 4:7$$

Substituting 4:7 in 4:3 we find that

$$\frac{dM}{dt} \equiv \left[\frac{\partial M}{\partial S} \cdot \frac{\partial F}{\partial M} \cdot \frac{dM}{dt} + \frac{\partial M}{\partial S} \cdot \frac{\partial F}{\partial \beta} \cdot \frac{d\beta}{dt} \right] + \frac{\partial M}{\partial \beta} \cdot \frac{d\beta}{dt}. \qquad 4:8$$

By inverse functions we know that

$$\frac{\partial M}{\partial S} \cdot \frac{\partial F}{\partial M} = 1.00. \qquad 4:9$$

Hence, by substitution in 4:8, we find that

$$0 = \frac{\partial M}{\partial S} \cdot \frac{\partial F}{\partial \beta} \cdot \frac{d\beta}{dt} + \frac{\partial M}{\partial \beta} \cdot \frac{d\beta}{dt}, \qquad 4:10$$

and

$$\frac{\partial M}{\partial S} \cdot \frac{\partial F}{\partial \beta} \cdot \frac{d\beta}{dt} = - \frac{\partial M}{\partial \beta} \cdot \frac{d\beta}{dt} = - \zeta(t). \qquad 4:11$$

Thus the second term in the bracket of formula 4:8 is equal to the inverse of the rate of saving by society as a whole; that is to say, it is equal to the rate of *anti-saving* by all traders. Furthermore, a comparison of 4:4 with 4:3 and 4:8 shows that the bracket term in formula 4:8 considered as a whole is equal to the rate of new receipts and also the rate of new expenditures. The rate of new receipts cannot be increased by savings on the part of society as a whole because the total rate of new receipts *won't* be kept constant by all traders while they are reducing their expenditures by saving. For the whole economy, receipts equal expenditures. This means that any increase in the supply of funds achieved by saving in the case of any one trader is bound to be offset by a reduction in the supply of funds somewhere else in the economy. Traders as a whole simply cannot increase their supply of funds by conserving their use of funds. The total rate of saving is concealed with a negative effect upon the rate of new receipts, as is shown by the presence of a term equal to $-\zeta$ in the bracketed part of formula 4:8.

Conservation of the existing supply of funds (saving) will *tend* to increase the total supply and will actually increase the supply of funds in the hands of some traders. It would cause an increase in the total supply were it not for the fact that one man's output (expenditure) of funds is another man's input (receipts), and vice versa. Conservation of funds by the whole economy merely means that traders are *trying* to increase their funds, but they succeed only in decreasing their rate of receipt of funds to an equivalent extent, without any increase in the total supply of funds resulting from their efforts.

But the effect of positive saving by society as a whole, while neutral with respect to the supply of funds, is devastating for the total flow of funds because the anti-savings are not in practice buffered in any great degree by the first of the two terms in formula 4:8, viz. $\frac{\partial M}{\partial S} \cdot \frac{\partial F}{\partial M} \cdot \frac{dM}{dt}$. The algebraic sign of the two partial derivatives is plus. Therefore, the triple product as a whole has the same sign as that of the total derivative, $\frac{dM}{dt}$, which is the rate of increase of the supply of funds caused by the creation of new funds. This is inclined to be of negative sign for psychological reasons when the sign of ζ is positive because people are conserving their funds.

In Chapter Three we developed the important formula

$$\frac{dY}{dt} \equiv [Z(t) - Z(t\text{-}K)] + \frac{dK}{dt} \cdot Z(t\text{-}K). \qquad 4:12$$

This formula says that the rate of increase of total capital, $\frac{dY}{dt}$, is equal to the rate of new income (bracket term) plus the rate of conservation of capital (differential term). This can be restated as

$$\frac{dY}{dt} \equiv \int_{t\text{-}K}^{t} \frac{dZ}{dt} \cdot dt + \sigma(t), \qquad 4:13$$

where the symbol σ stands for the rate of conservation of capital. It will be recalled that $Z(t)$ is the total rate of purchases (sales) of tangible goods and services. The Z term is therefore included in the S term in 4:11 because the latter is the total rate of receipt of funds from any source whatever. Now let us define the term V where

$$Z(t) = M(t).V(t). \qquad 4:14$$

Since Z is the total rate of purchase *and* sale of tangible goods and services, the term V is clearly the instantaneous rate of turnover of positively-valued funds arising from the purchase and sale of tangible goods and services. From differentiation of 4:14 we get

$$dZ = \frac{\partial Z}{\partial M} \cdot dM + \frac{\partial Z}{\partial V} \cdot dV \qquad 4:15$$

$$= VdM + MdV. \qquad 4:16$$

Substituting 4:16 in 4:13 we obtain the interesting result that

$$\frac{dY}{dt} \equiv \int_{t-K}^{t} V\frac{dM}{dt} dt + \int_{t-K}^{t} M\frac{dV}{dt} dt + \sigma(t). \qquad 4:17$$

We propose to show in a later chapter that the increase in value of tangible capital of all traders is equal to their rate of expenditure of new funds for tangible goods and personal services. The latter term is given by the first integral on the right of formula 4:17. Hence the net of the first two terms in 4:17 is equal to zero and we find that

$$\int_{t-K}^{t} M\frac{dV}{dt} dt = -\sigma(t). \qquad 4:18$$

Applying the theorem of the mean to this equation we can eliminate the integration sign, and we come up with the very powerful result that the rate of anti-conservation of capital, $-\sigma$, is given by the product of an average value of funds, $M(\xi)$, multiplied by the new velocity of funds in exchange for goods and services, as stated by the difference term $V(t) - V(t - K)$, viz.

$$-\sigma(t) = M(\xi) [V(t) - V(t-K)]. \qquad 4:19$$

At an earlier point in this chapter we developed this important evaluation of the rate of increase of the total supply of funds:

$$\frac{dM}{dt} = [S(t) - S(t-\beta)] + \frac{d\beta}{dt} S(t-\beta), \qquad 4:20$$

wherein, it will be recalled, $S(t)$ is the instantaneous rate of receipt of (positively-valued) funds, while $\beta(t)$ is the average historical period of turnover of all funds at time t. Reference to formulas 4:3 and 4:4 will show that 4:20 can also be written in this way:

$$\frac{dM}{dt} = [S(t) - S(t-\beta)] + \frac{\partial M}{\partial \beta} \cdot \frac{d\beta}{dt} \qquad 4:21$$

$$= \int_{t-\beta}^{t} \frac{dS}{dt} dt + \zeta(t), \qquad 4:22$$

wherein ζ has been designated as the total rate of saving, which is the differential term on the right of 4:21. Now let us define the term V_2 by the formula

$$S(t) \equiv M(t)V_2(t) \qquad 4:23$$

wherein V_2 is the average rate of turnover of funds in exchange for all things, tangible goods as well as other funds. It follows that

$$\frac{dS}{dt} \equiv \frac{\partial S}{\partial M} \cdot \frac{dM}{dt} + \frac{\partial S}{\partial V_2} \cdot \frac{dV_2}{dt} . \qquad 4:24$$

Hence by substitution of 4:24 in 4:22 we have this expression for rate of increase of the supply of funds:

$$\frac{dM}{dt} \equiv \left[\int_{t-\beta}^{t} \frac{\partial S}{\partial M} \cdot \frac{dM}{dt} \, dt + \int_{t-\beta}^{t} \frac{\partial S}{\partial V_2} \cdot \frac{dV_2}{dt} \, dt \right] + \varsigma(t). \qquad 4:25$$

The first integral in the bracket term can be written as

$$\frac{\partial M}{\partial S} \cdot \frac{\partial S}{\partial M} \cdot \frac{dM}{dt} = \frac{dM}{dt} . \qquad 4:26$$

Substituting in 4:25 and cancelling out $\dfrac{dM}{dt}$ we get

$$\int_{t-\beta}^{t} \frac{\partial S}{\partial V_2} \cdot \frac{dV_2}{dt} \, dt = - \varsigma(t), \qquad 4:27$$

while by 4:18 we know that

$$\int_{t-K}^{t} M \frac{dV}{dt} \, dt = - \sigma(t). \qquad 4:28$$

Solving the last two equations simultaneously we find that

$$\frac{\varsigma}{\sigma} \equiv \frac{\displaystyle\int_{t-\beta}^{t} \frac{\partial S}{\partial V_2} \cdot \frac{dV_2}{dt} dt}{\displaystyle\int_{t-K}^{t} M(t) \cdot \frac{dV}{dt} dt} \equiv \frac{M(\xi)\,[V_2(t) - V_2(t-\beta)]}{M'(\xi)\,[V(t) - V(t-K)]} . \qquad 4:29$$

It is mathematically possible that $M(\xi)$ should equal $M'(\xi)$ because they are both unspecified averages of M over a period of time.

Since $K > \beta$ while $V_2 > V$, it is possible for the two bracket terms in 4:29 to likewise be equal. In short it is possible that $\zeta/\sigma = 1.00$ and therefore that ζ, the total rate of saving, can be equal to σ, the total rate of conservation of capital. One would certainly expect that the conservation of funds would imply the conservation of goods. In any event it may be stated as an unproved hypothesis that ζ *tends* to equal σ so that the rate of saving *tends* to equal the rate of conservation of capital; that is

$$\zeta(t) \doteq \sigma(t). \qquad\qquad 4:30$$

In furtherance of the development of our model of business fluctuations it is necessary to distinguish the rate of new receipts from the rate of receipt or expenditure of new funds for tangible goods and services. The former is stated algebraically as follows:

$$R(t) \equiv [S(t) - S(t\text{-}\beta)] \qquad\qquad 4:31$$

where $R(t)$ is the rate of new receipts. That is to say, it is the amount by which the present rate of receipt of funds from all sources exceeds the rate at an earlier date, $t - \beta$. On the other hand, the rate of expenditure of new funds for tangible goods and services is given by the expression

$$\eta(t) \equiv \frac{\partial Y}{\partial Z} \cdot \frac{\partial Z}{\partial M} \cdot \frac{dM}{dt} \qquad\qquad 4:32$$

where η is the rate of expenditure of new funds for tangible goods and services; i.e., η is the contribution which the creation of new funds makes to the increase of capital by way of its effect on the total rate of purchase (sale) of tangible goods and services.

In this expression we run across an all-important dimensional operator, namely $\frac{\partial Y}{\partial Z}$. The partial derivative, $\frac{\partial Z}{\partial M}$, is—as reference to 4:16 will show—equal to V, the velocity of funds in exchange for tangible goods and services. The rate at which new funds are being created is given by the derivative, $\frac{dM}{dt}$, and is of the dimension dollars per period of time. The rate at which this instantaneous increment of funds is being spent for goods and services is the product of their velocity, V, and their rate of creation, $\dfrac{dM}{dt}$. This product is of the dimension dollars per period of time per period of time. However, it is necessary to equate the contribution of new funds to the rate of expenditure of new funds so conceived and the rate conceived as a variable of the dimension dollars per period of time. This change of dimension is achieved by multiplying $\dfrac{\partial Z}{\partial M} \cdot \dfrac{dM}{dt}$ by the partial derivative $\dfrac{\partial Y}{\partial Z}$, which is of the dimension period of time. This partial derivative may be replaced by a definite integral: *i.e.*, η can be written as

$$\eta(t) \equiv \int_{t-K}^{t} \frac{\partial Z}{\partial M} \cdot \frac{dM}{dt}\, dt = \int_{t-K}^{t} V \frac{dM}{dt}\, dt. \qquad 4{:}33$$

The interval of integration, K, may be regarded as the "interval of newness" just as it was regarded in the discussion of new income. The interval of newness enters into the argument again in the definition of anti-saving and therefore in the definition of saving, when it is written as

$$\sigma(t) = -\int_{t-K}^{t} M \frac{dV}{dt}\, dt \doteq \zeta(t). \qquad 4{:}34$$

Just how far back must the velocity of funds be carried in estimating the impact of a rate of change, $\dfrac{dV}{dt}$, in order to get the proper evaluation of saving by society as a whole? The answer to this question depends upon the variables to which it is desired to relate the rate of saving.

D. H. Robertson is one of the few economists who have faced this problem squarely, but the solution which he proposed seems rather obscure to us. He said that the correct interval of integration is an "economic day," and he defines an economic day not as a solar day of twenty-four hours but rather as that period of time which is (barely) so short that the firm is unable to make a substantial change in business commitments.[1]

This problem of finding the dimensional operator arises in business cycle theory whenever it is desired to express a rate having a single time dimension as a function of a rate having a double time dimension. The rate of investment, for example, cannot be expressed as a

---

[1] See D. H. Robertson, "Saving and Hoarding," *The Economic Journal*, September, 1933, p. 399.

function of the rate of change in the rate of total wages without the inclusion in the function of the *correct* dimensional operator for this particular situation, *i.e.*, the operator which converts dollars per period of time per period of time to simply dollars per period of time *in the given relationship*. The dimensional operator itself is a variable function of time, and its existence cannot be implied by any statement made by a writer on cycle theory, as might possibly be the case if the operator were a constant. Robertson merits respect for having recognized the existence of the problem, but his solution seems almost as transcendental as that given by medieval scholastics to the problem of how many angels could stand on the point of a needle.

Clark Warburton has given a somewhat more realistic answer to the problem. He has defined saving as the product of the money supply at any given time multiplied by the difference between the circuit velocity of money at its highest point in recent history and its velocity at the present time. Thus, if $V_3(t)$ is the "circuit" velocity of money expressed as a function of time and $M'(t)$ is the money supply while the peak of velocity was reached at time $t - \Delta$, Warburton defines $\zeta(t)$ as follows

$$\zeta(t) \equiv M'(t) \, [V_3(t\text{-}\Delta) - V_3(t)] . \qquad 4{:}35$$

In this definition he has (inadvertently) defined the interval of newness as being equal to Δ, because his definition can be restated as

$$\zeta(t) \equiv - M'(t) \int_{t-\Delta}^{t} \frac{dV_3}{dt} . \, dt. \qquad 4{:}36$$

It is necessary to put the minus sign in front of the restatement in order that there will be negative saving whenever the velocity is gaining and positive saving whenever the velocity of money is declining, as is called for by Warburton's definition. Warburton's formula has the obvious disadvantage of never being negative unless and until the present velocity exceeds the peak value of the past. It is also obvious that his interval of newness will get to become steadily larger so long as a new peak in velocity is not reached.

As we have said, the correct "interval of newness," or interval of integration, depends upon the nature of the variables which one desires to tie together. If it is desired to tie in the rate of new income with the rate of increase of capital, we have shown that K, the average period of turnover of tangible capital, is the proper interval. On the other hand, if a relationship is sought between total rate of saving and the supply of funds, the proper interval of integration is given by β, the average period of turnover of all funds in all kinds of transactions. This is seen by referring to formula 4:25 above, wherein the second definite integral is the rate of saving with the sign reversed, *viz.*

$$\zeta(t) = - \int_{t-\beta}^{t} \frac{\partial S}{\partial V_2} \cdot \frac{dV_2}{dt} dt \qquad\qquad 4:37$$

$$= - \int_{t-\beta}^{t} M(t) \frac{dV_2}{dt} dt \qquad\qquad 4:38$$

$$\dot{=} - M(\xi) [V_2(t) - V_2(t-\beta)]. \qquad\qquad 4:39$$

This last result is the same as that stated by Warburton's concept in 4:35 with two very important differences: (1) the interval of newness is given by $\beta(t)$, the average period of turnover of all funds, and (2) the other element in the product is not $M'(t)$, the total money supply at a point in time, but $M(\xi)$, which is an average value of the total supply of all funds on hand during the interval of newness, β.

On the other hand, if it is desired to relate the impact of saving in all kinds of funds (of which the money supply is only a part) to the increase of tangible capital, the integral of integration (interval of newness) is given by K, the average period of turnover of tangible capital (assuming that the rate of conservation of capital is about equal to the rate of saving) as shown by the formula

$$\zeta(t) \dot{=} - \int_{t-K}^{t} M(t) \frac{dV}{dt} dt \qquad\qquad 4:40$$

$$\dot{=} -M(\xi) [V(t) - V(t-K)]. \qquad\qquad 4:41$$

Chapter 5

SOME STATISTICAL RELATIONSHIPS
OF SAVINGS, INVESTMENT, AND
NEW INCOME

In the present chapter we turn to the statistical verification of the identities revealed in Chapter Three and, also, to such observational or empirical study of the behavior of savings, investment, and new income as is permitted by the degrees of freedom to be found within the identities. In making this statistical study we shall, of course, work with data for the United States, because the data for this area are most readily available and because they pertain to an area which approaches fairly closely the theoretical ideal of a great and largely self-contained economy.

The statistical data from original sources for this country are not the instantaneous rates with which we have found it most convenient to work in our theoretical analysis. Instead, these data are accumulations of rates over a finite period of time, usually a year. For our present purpose we have the choice of either converting our theoretical rates to the approximately equivalent accumulations or else converting the observed accumulations to approximately equivalent instantaneous rates in order to make the desired comparisons.

In accordance with our general policy of tampering with observational data as little as possible, we have elected to convert the instantaneous rates given by our theory to the approximate annual accumulations and then compare these results with observed behavior with no adjustment of data at all in most cases. In this way we shall be protected against any charge of manipulating or adjusting factual material in order to produce desired and possibly spurious results. An early physicist said, "Give me a long lever and I will move the world." In similar fashion, an economist might say, "give me leave to adjust the observations as much as I please and I will verify any theorem whatever."

If we rearrange equation 3:16 for the duration of a year, we obtain the following result, when ϵ represents a year's time:

$$\int_{\tau-\epsilon}^{\tau} \frac{dY}{dt} dt \equiv \left[\int_{\tau-\epsilon}^{\tau} Z(t) dt - \int_{\tau-\epsilon}^{\tau} Z(t-K_t) \, dt \right] + \int_{\tau-\epsilon}^{\tau} \frac{dK}{dt} Z(t-K_t) \, dt. \quad 5:1$$

This simply states that the increase of wealth during the year ending at time $t = \tau$ is equal to the new income received during that year plus the accumulated savings of that year. Once again, we are dealing with an identity or, if preferred, a "truism."

The exact value of the new income received during the year may be approximated by this expression, wherein I_τ represents accumulated new income for the year ending at $t = \tau$:

$$I_\tau = \int_{\tau-\epsilon}^{\tau} Z(t) \, dt - \int_{\tau-\bar{K}_{\tau}-\epsilon}^{\tau-\bar{K}_{\tau}} Z(t) \, dt. \quad 5:2$$

In this equation $\bar{K}_\tau$ represents an average value of K — the average period of turnover of tangible wealth — during the year ending at time $t = \tau$. In Chapter Two we employed the symbol Z_τ to designate the accumulated flow of funds (or sales of services and tangible goods) in the year ending at time $t = \tau$. Let us simplify our notation by allowing $Z_{\tau-K_\tau}$ to represent the second definite integral above. New income for the year ending at τ will then be approximately equal to total sales of the said year minus the total sales of a *twelve-month period* (not necessarily a calendar year) ending K_τ years earlier than time $t = \tau$.

In the simplified notation suggested

$$I_\tau = Z_\tau - Z_{\tau-K_\tau}. \quad 5:3$$

This gives us a workable formula for a statistical evaluation of I_τ, the new income of any calendar year. The Z_τ data can be taken directly from original sources. If the values of K_τ are computed for the end of each calendar year corresponding with Z_τ, a simple arithmetic mean of the K_τ's at τ and at $\tau-\epsilon$ will serve as an estimate of K_τ. We have then only to interpolate among the Z_τ data to find the value of $Z_{\tau-K_\tau}$.

For this latter purpose we shall employ a simple straight-line inter-polation. If K_T happens to be an integer, measured in years, the straight-line interpolation for Z_{T-K_T} involves no statistical error what-ever beyond that resulting from the simplified estimation of K_T itself. Thus, if K_T should happen to be exactly two years as of December 31, 1951, then the new income for the calendar year 1951 would be given very nearly by the following:

$$I_{51} = \int_{Dec.\ 31,\ 1950}^{Dec.\ 31,\ 1951} Z(t)\,dt - \int_{Dec.\ 31,\ 1948}^{Dec.\ 31,\ 1949} Z(t)\,dt. \qquad 5{:}4$$

$$I_{51} = Z_{51} - Z_{49}. \qquad 5{:}5$$

Because the values of Z_{51} and Z_{49} are available as direct observations, no error is caused by the straight-line interpolation itself, although there may be appreciable errors in the raw data for both 1951 and 1949, and in the estimated value of K_T.

The possible statistical error involved in a straight-line interpolation for Z_{T-K_T} increases as K_T ceases to be an integer, neglecting again any error in the estimation of K_T itself or in the raw data for calendar years. Thus, if K_T for December 31, 1951 should happen to be 2¾ years, straight-line interpolation would produce the following results:

$$I_{51} = \int_{Dec.\ 31,\ 1950}^{Dec.\ 31,\ 1951} Z(t)\,dt - \int_{Mar.\ 31,\ 1948}^{Mar.\ 31,\ 1949} Z(t)\,dt. \qquad 5{:}6$$

Direct observation for the twelve-month period called for by the second integral in 5:6 is not available, so we need an interpolation between the values for calendar 1949 and calendar 1948. By the straight-line method we shall take one-fourth of the total sales for 1949 and three-fourths of the total sales for 1948 as our interpolated value for Z_{T-K_T}, since one-fourth of the twelve-month period to be evaluated lies in the year 1949 and three-fourths of it lies in 1948. This involves an arbitrary statistical assumption which almost certain-ly is not exactly true, but it saves time in computation and is in any case a first approximation of the exact truth. It is also a good approximation, we think, because the results obtained in this manner coincide very closely with the values required to satisfy the identities which we know would have to obtain if our computations were exact.

In practice, of course, the statistical evaluation of new income as just described requires the preliminary estimate of the values of K_T for the end of each calendar year. This, in turn, rests upon the definitive equation for K_T, as stated in Chapter Three, *viz.*:

$$Y_T \equiv \int_{T\text{-}K_T}^{T} Z(t)\, dt , \qquad\qquad 3:1$$

wherein the "known values" are specified as $Y(\tau)$, the total value of tangible wealth at the end of the year τ and, as before in this work, $Z(t)$, the instantaneous rate of total flow of funds in exchange for services and tangible goods.

The procedure we follow is to estimate the values of Y_T first and then, by a process of linear interpolation among the values of Z_T, to calculate K_T. And to evaluate the Y_T's we first compute ΔY_T, the accumulated changes in total wealth for each calendar year, and then chain the ΔY_T's together to obtain the values of Y_T, starting of course with an estimated value of Y_T for the first of the thirty-six years we have selected for observation and study. ΔY_T is, of course, simplified notation for the definite integral on the left side of equation 3:16, *viz.*:

$$\Delta Y_T \equiv \int_{T\text{-}\epsilon}^{T} \frac{dY}{dt}\, dt . \qquad\qquad 5:7$$

With the ΔY_T values in hand and also Y_T for the initial period, the evaluation of the other Y_T's is a matter of simple arithmetic, *viz.*:

$$Y_2 = Y_1 + \Delta Y_2 \qquad\qquad 5:8a$$

$$Y_3 = Y_2 + \Delta Y_3 \qquad\qquad 5:8b$$

$$\vdots \qquad \vdots \qquad \vdots$$

$$Y_{36} = Y_{35} + \Delta Y_{36} . \qquad\qquad 5:8c$$

We use this method because there is no annual census of wealth. If there were, our "build-up" method of obtaining Y_T would be unnecessary. Data for Y_T would be ready to hand and we would derive the accumulated change in wealth for each year by subtracting these data successively.

The estimates of the changes in wealth which are necessary to the method actually used are based upon a relationship which will be explained below in Chapter Nine. From the discussion of this later chapter it will appear that the relationship between national income and the change in national wealth in a given period may be stated as follows:

$$G_T = \frac{Z_T}{\mu} + \frac{m}{\mu} \cdot \Delta Y_T. \qquad 5:9$$

In this equation, G is the "national income" for the year ending at T Z_T is total sales (or gross income), ΔY_T (equal to γ_T) is the change in total wealth, m is the number of stages of production (to be explained in Chapter Six) and $\mu = m + 1$, or a wage-multiplier.[1]

By means of an adaptation of the Department of Commerce data, we obtain estimated values for G_T for each year under study, and from Chapter Six below we obtain values for μ and m. Utilizing the Federal Reserve Board's data for Z_T and those of Robert R. Doane and Clark Warburton (sources noted in Chapter Two), we estimate the annual changes in the value of tangible wealth by means of a transposition of equation 5:9 as follows:

$$\Delta Y_T = \frac{\mu G_T - Z_T}{m} = \gamma_T, \qquad 5:10$$

where γ_T is accumulated investment for the year and therefore must be identically equal to the change in total wealth, as we have shown in Chapter Three.

The values for the annual increases of tangible wealth or (what comes to the same thing) the investment for the various years, obtained in this way, are presented in Table 3. Also shown are the values of total wealth computed by "chaining" these increments together and attaching them to the value of total wealth at the end of the year 1920, as given by R. R. Doane and others in the references made above.

All of the values in this table are positive. This is certain to be true with respect to the data for total wealth, because there could

---

[1]The "national income" as conceived in this work is not exactly the same thing as either "national income" or "gross national product" as these concepts are defined by the United States Department of Commerce, but it is an aggregate which is a "first cousin" to both. The reasons for developing our theory in terms of a modification of the concepts of the Department of Commerce will be explained in Chapter Eight in the course of the development of our own concept of "national income." But for the purposes of the present chapter we will employ the Department of Commerce data (as quoted in the Federal Reserve Bulletin, *passim*) for national income because, as a practical matter, nothing better is available as original or source material. The use of these data will give us first approximations for ΔY_T, by substitution in 5:9.

TABLE 3

ESTIMATED VALUES OF INVESTMENT DURING THE YEAR
AND OF TOTAL TANGIBLE WEALTH AT THE END
OF THE YEAR IN THE UNITED STATES, 1921-1956

Year	Estimated Investment (Billions of Dollars)	Estimated Value of Total Tangible Wealth (Billions of Dollars)
1921	+27.0	494.8*
1922	+27.5	522.3
1923	+32.6	554.9
1924	+31.5	586.4
1925	+32.7	619.1
1926	+35.3	654.4
1927	+32.0	687.3
1928	+33.6	720.9
1929	+36.5	757.4
1930	+35.9	793.3
1931	+25.3	818.6
1932	+17.2	835.8
1933	+18.6	854.4
1934	+24.2	878.6
1935	+24.7	903.3
1936	+31.4	934.7
1937	+31.4	966.1
1938	+29.3	995.4
1939	+33.0	1,028.4
1940	+38.4	1,066.8
1941	+51.9	1,118.7
1942	+75.0	1,193.7
1943	+93.5	1,287.2
1944	+95.5	1,382.7
1945	+87.7	1,470.4
1946	+74.7	1,545.1
1947	+75.4	1,620.5
1948	+90.9	1,711.4
1949	+89.6	1,801.0
1950	+97.9	1,898.9
1951	+119.3	2,018.2
1952	+121.7	2,139.9
1953	+131.5	2,271.4
1954	+126.6	2,398.0
1955	+143.1	2,541.1
1956	+158.3	2,699.4

*The original value for tangible wealth (the value for 1920) was obtained by a compromise between the estimate of R. R. Doane for that year in *The Measurement of American Wealth* and the estimate of the National Industrial Conference Board for that year, as quoted by Doane in the work cited, p. 9.

not be less than no total wealth. But it is noteworthy that the increments of wealth are all positive. Even in 1932, at the very bottom of the worst depression in the history of this country, there was at least a slight positive investment rather than a disinvestment or negative investment.

The explanation of this paradox, if indeed it is a paradox, lies in the fact that we have measured the value of wealth at cost to the owners and not at the market. Thousands of farms, for example, are valued by our reckoning at what they cost the people who owned them in 1932 and not at the values which they would have fetched if they had been thrown on the market in that year. To be sure, many farms *were* thrown on the market in 1932 and were sold at a large loss. Such losses tended to pull down the total wealth aggregate valued at cost to the owners, and tended in themselves toward making investment negative. However, many other farmers, though sorely pressed by their creditors, were able to hold on to their properties and thereby to sustain the value of Y_τ for the whole country. And the quantities of "new" goods sold in 1932 were sufficient, even though sold at depressed unit prices, to contribute a small gain, on net balance, in total wealth.[2] From this salient point and from certain other vital considerations which we will survey at a later point in this work, one might infer that, if new investment should ever become negative for as long as one whole year, the end of private capitalism in any country would be at hand.

Since the value of K_τ has never been less than a year in the period of 36 years which we are using for statistical observation, and since ϵ denotes an interval of one year, equation 3:1 above may be expanded to read:

$$Y_\tau \equiv \int_{\tau-\epsilon}^{\tau} Z(t)\,dt + \int_{\tau-2\epsilon}^{\tau-\epsilon} Z(t)\,dt \ldots + \int_{\tau-i\epsilon}^{\tau-i\epsilon+\epsilon} Z(t)\,dt + \int_{\tau-i\epsilon-j\epsilon}^{\tau-i\epsilon} Z(t)\,dt, \quad 5\!:\!11$$

where i is the number of the last *full* year extending backward in time (including the number one year ending at time $t = \tau$) whose sales must be included with those of later years to produce a numerical total equal to the value of total wealth at time τ, and $j\epsilon$ is the

---

[2] Professor Schumpeter has remarked on what he called the "strange" phenomenon of the comparatively mild decline in total capital (valued at the market) during the worst of all business depressions.

fraction of another year, beyond the last full year, whose sales must be so included as determined by straight-line interpolation. Putting the matter in another way, $i\epsilon + j\epsilon = K_T$.

When $j\epsilon = O$, it is easy to see that equation 5:11 produces a ready estimate of K_T. Let us say that the sales for the last three years (including the one ending at $t = \tau$) are exactly equal to total wealth at τ. Then we add $Z_T + Z_{T-1} + Z_{T-2}$ and we note that $Y_T > Z_T + Z_{T-1}$, but that $Z_T + Z_{T-1} + Z_{T-2} = Y_T$. We therefore conclude that $K_T = 3\epsilon = 3$ years. When K is an integer, no error is involved in its estimation beyond the errors already present in the data for Z and Y.

However, if we note that $Z_T + Z_{T-1} + Z_{T-2} < Y_T$ but $Z_T + Z_{T-1} + Z_{T-2} + Z_{T-3} > Y_T$, we know that $K_T < 4 > 3$ years. At this point we employ straight-line interpolation to estimate the value of K_T. If we had daily data for total sales we could avoid interpolation by an arbitrary formula because we could go on adding daily data for total sales to the sum of $Z_T + Z_{T-1} + Z_{T-2}$ until the result was exactly equal to Y_T. If this occurred on September 30 of the year ending at $\tau - 3$, we could evaluate K_T as about 3 years and 90 days, or perhaps 3¼ years.

Since we have only annual data available, we resort to straight-line interpolation as a practical solution for our problem. Assume that Y_T is $900 billion and that $Z_T + Z_{T-1} + Z_{T-2}$ amount to $850 billion. Then we have a remainder of $50 billion to be accounted for by sales in the fourth year (counting backward). If sales in the fourth year (counting backward) were $200 billion, by straight-line interpolation we would estimate that one-fourth of these sales came in the last three months of this fourth year. We would estimate K_T to be the first three years counting backward plus one-fourth of the fourth year, or 3¼ years altogether. Then $i\epsilon$ in equation 5:11 would be three years and $j\epsilon$ would be one-fourth year, while $\tau - i\epsilon - j\epsilon$ would be $\tau - 3¼$ years, and $K_T = i\epsilon + j\epsilon = 3¼$ years. The upper limit on the last definite integral on the right-hand side of equation 5:11 would be $\tau - 3$ years.

Utilizing the statistical methods just described, the data for Y_T shown in Table 3 above, and the data for Z_T obtained from the reference sources mentioned above, we have computed values for K_T in the United States for the end of each of the 36 years used in our study. These values of K_T and the values of Y_T and Z_T from which they were derived appear in Table 4.

TABLE 4

APPROXIMATE VALUES OF K_T, Z_T, AND Y_T
IN THE UNITED STATES, 1921-1956

Year	Average Period of Turnover of Tangible Wealth K_T (Years)	Total Sales of Services and Tangible Goods in Calendar Year Z_T (Billion Dollars)	Total Value of Tangible Wealth at End of Year Y_T (Billion Dollars)
1921	1.97	221.1	494.8
1922	2.18	249.3	522.3
1923	2.11	281.6	554.9
1924	2.04	293.2	586.4
1925	2.01	323.5	619.1
1926	1.96	338.7	654.4
1927	2.02	342.5	687.3
1928	2.04	365.2	720.9
1929	2.05	376.4	757.4
1930	2.31	304.8	793.3
1931	2.72	242.6	818.6
1932	3.27	185.3	835.8
1933	3.84	171.6	854.4
1934	4.25	203.3	878.6
1935	4.44	237.0	903.3
1936	4.28	270.5	934.7
1937	3.82	297.1	966.1
1938	3.66	267.9	995.4
1939	3.60	308.0	1,028.4
1940	3.53	336.6	1,066.8
1941	3.22	415.8	1,118.7
1942	2.83	500.2	1,193.7
1943	2.45	601.4	1,287.2
1944	2.22	659.8	1,382.7
1945	2.21	677.0	1,470.4
1946	2.17	747.3	1,545.1
1947	1.98	866.4	1,620.5
1948	1.88	936.9	1,711.4
1949	1.93	926.1	1,801.0
1950	1.93	1,036.4	1,898.9
1951	1.82	1,173.0	2,018.2
1952	1.77	1,235.3	2,139.9
1953	1.80	1,290.0	2,271.4
1954	1.87	1,279.3	2,398.0
1955	1.90	1,393.4	2,541.1
1956	1.86	1,303.7	2,699.4

Once values of K_T have been estimated in the manner indicated, $\bar{K}_T$ may be approximated by taking the simple arithmetic mean of K_T and $K_{T-\epsilon}$ for each year. Once again we can employ a straight-line interpolation as an approximation of the values which we seek, which in the next stage of our study are the values of Z_{T-K_T} from the equation.

$$Z_{T-K_T} \doteq \int_{T-\bar{K}_{T-\epsilon}}^{T-\bar{K}_T} Z(t)\, dt. \qquad\qquad 5{:}12$$

The straight-line interpolation for Z_{T-K} is a matter of simple arithmetic, as applied to the raw data for Z_T in the several years. When K_T is an integer, the arithmetic is very simple indeed. Suppose, for example, $K_T = 2\epsilon = 2$ years for the year 1951. Then to find Z_{T-K} for the calendar year 1951 we go back in time two years earlier than the end of this calendar year, which will be December 31, 1949, and add the flow of funds for twelve months prior to December 31, 1949. In other words, Z_{T-K} for calendar 1951 would simply be the total flow of funds for the calendar year 1949 under the assumed circumstances. Z_{T-K_T} for 1951 would equal Z_T for 1949.

If $\bar{K}_T$ turned out to be 2.5 years and if the data for the flow of funds were available by months, we would add the flow for the first six months of 1949 to the flow for the last six months of 1948 to obtain the value of Z_{T-K_T} for 1951. That is, Z_{T-K_T} for 1951 would be the total sales of services and tangible goods for an uninterrupted twelve-month period evenly divided between 1948 and 1949.

Since actual data are available only by years, we have in practice to approximate the total sales for this twelve-month period which overlaps the two consecutive years 1948 and 1949. We elect to do this by straight-line interpolation, which means that we will add half of the total sales of calendar 1949 to half of the total sales for 1948, under the assumed circumstances. If $\bar{K}_T$ should happen to be 2.25 years, we would add three-fourths of the total sales for 1949 to one-fourth of the total sales for 1948, and proceed in similar fashion whenever $\bar{K}_T$ is a mixed number.

The values of Z_T as given by R. R. Doane and the Federal Reserve Board, and the values of Z_{T-K} for the corresponding years as computed by the method just explained, are shown in Table 5 for the United States during the period of 36 years which we are using for

TABLE 5

THE TOTAL FLOW OF FUNDS IN THE UNITED STATES
FOR CERTAIN CALENDAR YEARS AND FOR TWELVE-
MONTH PERIODS K_T YEARS EARLIER, AND NEW
INCOME FOR THE SAME CALENDAR YEARS

Year	Flow of Funds in the United States Z_T (Billion Dollars)	Flow of Funds for a Twelve-Month Period K_T Years Earlier Z_{T-K_T} (Billion Dollars)	New Income in the United States I_T (Billion Dollars)
1921	221.1	264.4	-43.3
1922	249.3	279.6	-30.3
1923	281.6	227.9	+53.7
1924	293.2	248.2	+45.0
1925	323.5	281.3	+42.2
1926	338.7	294.4	+44.3
1927	342.5	322.9	+19.6
1928	365.2	338.1	+27.1
1929	376.4	342.3	+34.1
1930	304.8	358.2	-53.4
1931	242.6	368.3	-125.7
1932	185.3	373.4	-188.1
1933	171.6	364.9	-193.3
1934	203.3	322.7	-119.4
1935	237.0	270.0	-33.0
1936	270.5	201.3	+69.2
1937	297.1	177.3	+119.8
1938	267.9	214.8	+53.1
1939	308.0	250.4	+57.6
1940	336.6	283.0	+53.6
1941	415.8	274.3	+141.5
1942	500.2	312.9	+197.1
1943	601.4	380.2	+221.2
1944	659.8	481.6	+178.2
1945	677.0	580.1	+96.9
1946	747.3	649.9	+97.4
1947	866.4	677.0	+189.4
1948	939.9	761.6	+178.3
1949	926.1	867.9	+58.2
1950	1,036.4	938.5	+97.9
1951	1,173.0	949.2	+223.8
1952	1,235.3	1,070.6	+164.7
1953	1,290.0	1,187.3	+102.7
1954	1,279.3	1,244.1	+35.2
1955	1,393.4	1,288.6	+104.8
1956	1,503.7	1,300.9	+202.8

observation and study. The difference between Z_T and Z_{T-K}, it will be remembered, is the value of accumulated new income, I_T, for any given calendar year. Accordingly, these differences have been computed and are also shown in Table 5.

A study of this table reveals some significant aspects of business fluctuations during the period of 36 years. In the first place, it will be noted that the new income of this country exhibited both positive and negative values in the pre-Rooseveltian era. On the other hand, since the time when the New Deal got well under way, there has never been a year in which new income was negative. A negative new income means, of course, that the (gross) income of the nation is actually lower in a given period of twelve months than it was in a twelve-month period some two, three, or four years earlier, depending on the value of K_T.

A negative new income also means that the economy is in the depression phase of the business cycle. This is shown clearly by the fact that new income was negative in 1921 and 1922, which were relatively depressed years after World War I, but positive in the expansionary years of 1923 and after. New income became negative again in 1930, the first full year of the great depression, and remained negative through 1935, reaching a negative maximum in 1933 and declining in negative value in 1934 and 1935 as the "pump-priming" operations of the Roosevelt administration began to take effect. Since 1935, new income has always been positive, and it reached a maximum positive value in 1943 at the peak of the stimulus provided by the military production of World War II. Does this unbroken string of 21 years of positive-valued new income mean that the secret of perpetual prosperity for this country has been discovered by Congress and the fiscal and financial leaders of the federal government?

Another noteworthy feature of the statistics of new income, as shown in Table 5, is the great fidelity with which they reflect even the minor cyclical fluctuations in business (the "recessions") as well as the larger cyclical fluctuations, or "booms" and "depressions." And it should be remembered that this has been achieved without any correction or adjustment of the data for secular trend.

This cyclical fidelity stands out clearly in Figure 1, in which the data for new income have been plotted without adjustment. The cyclical improvement which began in 1922 is shown by a rise in the curve representing I_T and the culmination of this post-war expansion in 1923 is reflected by the peak of I_T in that year. The recession or minor depression of 1927 is clearly indicated on the graph, as is also the recovery which lasted through 1929, when the crash in the stock market occurred.

The deepening depression after 1929 is rather accurately portrayed, as is the magical improvement of 1934, together with the lack of complete recovery at that time. The depression of 1937-1938 stands out well, and so does the failure of the Roosevelt administration to obtain more than a mediocre sort of recovery until the rearmament program was well under way in 1941. The tremendous stimulus of federal spending during the war is recorded, together with a post-war slump.

Of course, someone may ask whether it is at all remarkable that changes in new income, derived from changes in the total flow of funds, should give us an accurate picture of cyclical fluctuations in the economy. It seems to us that there is something remarkable about the accuracy with which our changes in new income measure the cyclical fluctuations in business. The reason for this opinion is that our figures for new income are not at all the same thing as the *first differences* of the annual data on the total flow of funds. It is, of course, a matter of elementary statistics that the taking of first differences of annual data will *tend* to remove the trend. And, since there is no seasonal variation at all in annual data, it follows that the first differences contain practically nothing except cyclical and irregular fluctuations (if the trend is linear). Thus first differences in annual data for the total flow of funds would be expected to show cyclical fluctuations rather well.

Our data for new income are also purified rather thoroughly of the irregular fluctuations, which may be considerable in unadjusted dollar-value series over the years. And the reason that irregular fluctuations are distilled out of our data is precisely that these data are *not* the first differences of the total flow of funds. New income is not this year's flow minus last year's flow, nor even this year's flow minus that of two years ago necessarily. The new income data show the difference between the total flow of funds in given years and the flow *at a variable time* in the past, the elapsed interval or lag of time being equal to the average period of turnover of total wealth, which shows a variation all the way from 4.44 years to as little as 1.77 years.

It is the effect of this variable time-lag that does the trick and gives us such a dependable picture of cyclical fluctuations—much more dependable than would be obtained by taking the simple first differences of Z_T. For example, the first differences would indicate that there was a complete recovery in 1922, whereas the data for new income show that there was only a lessening of the depression of 1921. Again, the first differences of Z_T indicate complete recovery in 1934, whereas the figure for new income in 1934 had a large negative value, albeit a much smaller negative value than it had in 1933. The figures for new income suggest that there was an improvement in business generally in 1934, but by no means a complete recovery. From other data available on the subject one would think this to be a more accurate summary of the situation in 1934 than it would be to pronounce it a year of recovery. And the same considerations apply to 1935, as can be seen from the data in Table 5.

The fact that the data for I_T give us so faithful a picture of cyclical fluctuations indicates rather convincingly that our concept of new income is not merely a difference term, resulting from a process of mathematical differentiation, which has no particular economic meaning. On the contrary, the statistical evidence shows the logic of our thinking about the concept of new income to be correct in two important respects: (a) that the rate of receipt of new income must be obtained by integrating over time a continuous variable which has a double time dimension (that is, dollars per period of time per period of time) and (b) that the "correct" interval of integration is given by the average period of turnover of all wealth, which is the interval we have employed in computing the new income of the nation statistically.

This interval of integration is "correct" in that its use results in an excellent—perhaps the most excellent—measure of cyclical fluctuations. It is also the correct interval in the further sense that it is the dimensional operator which must be employed in order that the changes in the rate of income may be expressed as a function of the rate of increase of wealth—a relationship which is fundamental to an understanding of business cycles.

As we have demonstrated in Chapter Four, the rate of savings can be computed by subtracting the rate of new income from the rate of increase of wealth, or from the rate of investment, which is the same thing for society as a whole. In our statistical work on this point, we have elected to work with annual accumulations rather than with instantaneous rates, because the data are more readily available in that form.

Let σ_T represent the savings accumulated during the year ending at time $t = \tau$, so that, as a matter of definition:

$$\sigma_T \equiv \int_{\tau-\epsilon}^{\tau} \sigma(t)\, dt .$$

5:13

Then

$$\sigma_T \equiv \gamma_T - I_T .$$

5:14

Data for γ_T, the accumulated investment for each year, have been given in Table 3 above, and data for I_T, the accumulated new income for each year, in Table 5. We proceed then to estimate σ_T, the accumulated savings, by simple subtraction, and we obtain the values for σ_T shown in Table 6.

There is another way in which σ_T can be computed statistically, which may be called the "direct" method, as opposed to the "indirect" method just described. By definition, the instantaneous *rate* of savings, $\sigma(t)$, for the whole economy is given by the following equation:

$$\sigma(t) \equiv Z(t-K_t) \frac{dK}{dt} .$$

5:15

An approximation of σ_T, the accumulated savings in a calendar year, is therefore given by

$$\sigma_T = Z_{T-K_T} \cdot \frac{1}{\epsilon} \Delta K_T ,$$

5:16

wherein Z_{T-K_T} is the total flow of funds in a certain period, as described above in this chapter, and ΔK_T is equal to $K_T - K_{T-\epsilon}$, or the difference between the value of K at the end of the given year and its value at the end of the preceding year. The values of ΔK_T are given by taking first differences of the values of K_T shown in Table 4, while the values of Z_{T-K_T} are taken directly from Table 5. Multiplication of these two sets of values gives estimated values of σ_T by the direct method, and these estimates are shown in Table 6, along with the values obtained by the indirect method.

If there were no errors in our interpolation devices, the values of σ_T obtained by the two methods should be identical. Comparison of

TABLE 6

ACCUMULATED SAVINGS IN THE UNITED STATES IN CALENDAR YEARS
AS COMPUTED BY DIFFERENT FORMULAE

Year	Investment Minus New Income as Estimated From the Formula $\sigma_T = \gamma_T - I_T$ (Billion Dollars)	Accumulated Savings as Estimated From the Formula $\sigma_T = \dfrac{\Delta K_T \cdot Z_{T-K_T}}{\epsilon}$ (Billion Dollars)
1921	+70.3	N.A.
1922	+57.8	+58.7
1923	-21.1	-16.0
1924	-13.8	-11.3
1925	-9.5	-11.8
1926	-9.0	-14.7
1927	+13.3	+19.4
1928	+6.3	+6.6
1929	+1.8	+3.4
1930	+89.3	+93.1
1931	+151.0	+151.0
1932	+205.3	+205.4
1933	+211.9	+208.0
1934	+143.6	+132.3
1935	+57.7	+51.3
1936	-37.8	-32.2
1937	-88.4	-87.0
1938	-23.8	-25.6
1939	-24.6	-27.7
1940	-15.2	-19.8
1941	-89.6	-85.0
1942	-122.1	-122.0
1943	-127.7	-144.5
1944	-82.7	-96.8
1945	-4.1	-5.8
1946	-22.7	-20.8
1947	-114.0	-115.1
1948	-87.4	-91.4
1949	+31.4	+34.9
1950	0.0	0.0
1951	-104.5	-104.4
1952	-43.0	-42.8
1953	+28.8	+23.7
1954	+91.4	+87.1
1955	+38.2	+38.6
1956	-60.0	-51.8

the results obtained by the two methods does not constitute a "verification" of economic theory, but instead furnishes a test of the consistency of the interpolation methods which we have employed. There may be errors in the original compilations but, if the arbitrary simplifications employed in order to interpolate are fairly self-consistent, the results obtained by the two methods should not be greatly different.

It would be more difficult than it would be worth to prove mathematically that our interpolation formulae are compensatory. Let it suffice to apply the empirical test of comparison of the observational results obtained. The two estimates of savings year by year, as shown in Table 6 and in Figure 2, are not identical but they do run remarkably close in most years. It will be noted that the algebraical *sign* of savings is not significantly different for the two estimates in any year, and in many years the numerical values are almost the same. In 1931, the two estimates were identical. In 1922, there is a difference of only 1.5 percent in the two estimates, and in 1932 there is a difference of only $100 million out of $150 billion.

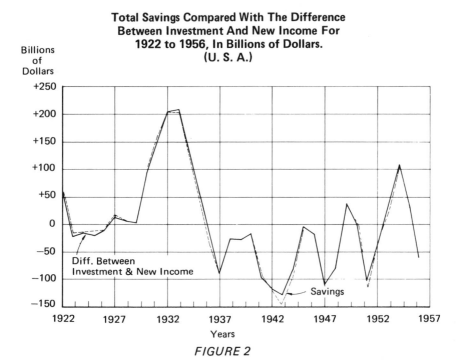

FIGURE 2

If our estimates of savings seem almost incredibly high in some years, it should be recalled that our concept of savings has only a correlative connection with the "orthodox" conception. That is, our savings are not supposed to equal the sum of the increases in savings deposits, securities owned, and so on. On the contrary, we have defined savings as the increase of total funds expended which *would* have taken place *if* new income had remained constant. Stated differently, it is the amount by which all traders in the economy *tried* to increase their funds by conserving the utilization of their capital or their funds. These attempted savings can and on occasion do run to many billions of dollars more than the actual increase of wealth when there is a large change in (gross) income or in the total flow of funds.

The important thing to note about savings, however, is that savings tend to be negatively correlated with the cyclical fluctuations in total business because they are almost perfectly correlated (negatively) with new income. When the algebraic sign of savings is reversed (thereby producing the values of anti-savings) there is not a single year in the entire period of 36 years under study in which the direction of the movement of anti-savings and new income is significantly different, as may be seen at a glance from Figure 1.

We also note in Figure 1 that there is virtually no secular trend visible in the graph of savings with the algebraic sign reversed, which are, of course, the anti-savings of the economy. The lack of secular trend in savings is also suggested by the fact that net savings (positive savings minus negative savings) for the 36 years amount to only +95 billions out of an aggregate value of $2282 billions. Another year or so of prosperity after 1956 almost surely reduced the net savings to zero for the entire period since 1921.

Since the savings represent variations in psychological attitudes (for reasons to be discussed later) which cause both positive and negative values to be generated in the economy, one would expect the secular trend to be zero indefinitely in an expanding economy. For reasons which are not altogether clear, people as a whole do not go on getting more optimistic without limit or more pessimistic without limit with regard to the conservation of their capital or the rate of utilization of their wealth. After so long a time there always comes a shift in attitude.

The impelling cause of a shift in attitude may be in part endogenous and in part exogenous, partly institutional or "external" and partly an aspect of the nervous mechanism of human beings. The endogenous part of the total behavior may be due not only to instability of emotional attitudes but also to the cumulative effect of decisions made at one time upon decisions made at another time. There is also a maximum positive value for the change in K_T from one year to the next, because $\frac{dK}{dt}$ must have a value of less than +1.00 if positive.

Unlike savings, the new income variable in Figure 1 does have a noticeable upward trend. This is certainly due to the presence of an upward trend of investment, because new income equals investment plus anti-savings (savings with algebraic sign reversed) and, if there is no secular trend in savings, there must be a trend in the other variable which, together with savings, gives the value of new income. The upward trend in investment exists because investment never has a negative value and its positive value is given an upward thrust as income expands. Indeed, investment is a function of (gross) income and K and, if K has no trend, investment must have an upward trend in order that income may expand, or vice versa the dollar value of income must expand if the dollar value of investment is to show a long-term increase.

The upward trend of new income will, in the course of time, reduce the magnitude of the correlation coefficient connecting new income with savings below its value of r = -0.70 for the period under observation here. However, this reduction in the value of the correlation as time goes on must be regarded as a defect of the Pearsonian coefficient of correlation as a measure of the degree of dependence between two variables. In this case an ever-increasing degree of "spuriously low" correlation will be reported by the value of the correlation coefficient connecting new income with the rate of saving as time goes on.[3]

---

[3]Textbooks on statistics usually give the impression that auto-correlation always produces spuriously *high* correlation between two time series. This is unfortunate. Take the case of the correlation between the production of oats in the United States and the deflated price of oats over the period of 35 years ending in 1914. There is high auto-correlation in the production series but only moderate auto-correlation in the price data. The correlation coefficient connecting the two series of data is zero if no adjustment is made for trend. This would indicate that there is no relationship between the production of oats and their price.

If we reduce the auto-correlation in the production series by adjusting the data for secular trend and then correlate the trend-adjusted data for production with the price data, the correlation rises (numerically) from zero to -0.80. This agrees with the common-sense conclusion that the production of oats and the price thereof are closely and negatively (inversely) correlated. Obviously, the auto-correlation in the production series introduced a spurious *lack* of correlation between production and price.

The *net* Pearsonian correlation between new income uncorrected for trend and savings uncorrected for trend may be computed with the rate of investment "held constant." Because the identity exists

$$I_T \equiv -\sigma_T + \gamma_T,$$ 5:17

the net correlation coefficient, $r_{I\sigma.\gamma}$, will always be nearly -1.00. Any slight deviation from this value which is obtained by statistical observation will be entirely due to faulty observation or inaccurate interpolation. Thus we reach the inescapable conclusion that saving by society as a whole is first, last, and always synonymous with recession or depression.

It is obvious from Figure 1 that the maximum correlation between new income and savings is to be found on the basis of zero lag. From one point of view this is a disadvantage, because an extremely high correlation is of doubtful value for purposes of prediction if the lag factor is zero. However, the simultaneity of the relationship does not detract from its value in connection with the question of control.

If one could obtain control of the savings of society in some fashion or other, one could control almost perfectly the cyclical fluidity of new income (and therefore to a high degree the cycles in gross income). And, of course, control of investment would control perfectly the *trend* of new income. In theory, at least, the regulation of cycles in savings plus the regulation of the secular trend in investment would in turn produce an almost perfect control of the new income of the economy, cycles and trend included. We shall return to the matter of the implications of our theory with respect to governmental control at a later point in this work. For the present it may be said that the possibility of controlling the rate of savings by means of governmental manipulation of investment through its fiscal and monetary policies would not seem to be promising. The reason is that there does not seem to be any large amount of correlation between saving and investment.

In order to measure the correlation between saving and investment it was necessary to adjust the investment data for trend, for reasons just discussed. This adjustment was obtained by taking deviations of the raw data from a simple linear trend fitted by the method of least squares. This simple linear trend might not be a serviceable

TABLE 7

INVESTMENT ADJUSTED FOR TREND IN THE UNITED STATES

Year	Adjusted Investment (Deviations from a Linear Trend) (Billion Dollars)	Variations in Investment Adjusted for Trend (Billion Dollars)
1921	+26.4	— —
1922	+23.3	-3.1
1923	+24.8	+1.5
1924	+20.1	-4.7
1925	+17.7	-2.4
1926	+16.8	-0.9
1927	+10.8	-6.0
1928	+7.9	-2.9
1929	-7.2	-0.7
1930	+2.9	-4.3
1931	-11.2	-14.1
1932	-22.9	-11.7
1933	-25.0	-2.1
1934	-23.1	+1.9
1935	-26.2	-3.1
1936	-24.0	+2.2
1937	-27.4	-3.4
1938	-32.3	-4.9
1939	-32.2	+0.1
1940	-30.4	+1.8
1941	-20.5	+9.9
1942	-1.0	+19.5
1943	+13.9	+14.9
1944	+12.3	-1.6
1945	+0.9	-11.4
1946	-15.7	-16.6
1947	-18.6	-2.9
1948	-6.6	+12.0
1949	-11.9	-5.3
1950	-6.8	+5.1
1951	+10.9	+17.7
1952	+9.8	-1.1
1953	+16.0	+6.2
1954	+10.2	-5.8
1955	+13.7	+3.5
1956	+25.5	+11.8

way of projecting investment in the very long run (that is, a linear trend may be of no service as a prediction of the future). However, for the purpose of measuring the correlation between the fluctuations of saving and investment in our period of 36 years, it is useful if not completely satisfactory. The data for investment adjusted for trend are shown in Table 7.

A fairly large negative correlation between savings and investment adjusted for trend is readily discoverable, but a more significant relationship is that between variations in savings and variations in investment adjusted for trend. The data for variations of investment adjusted for trend are also shown in Table 7 and are plotted in Figure 3. For present purposes we view the annual first differences in savings as measuring variations in savings, and these data are also plotted in Figure 3. The rather mediocre negative correlation which exists between variations of savings and variations of investment adjusted for trend is clearly shown in this chart. The correlation coefficient has an algebraical value of -0.55. Although not a high correlation, it is nevertheless significant at a level of one percent.

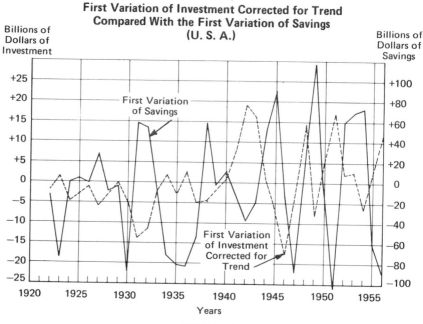

FIGURE 3

Fluctuations in investment adjusted for trend seem to be associated loosely with fluctuations in the opposite direction in savings. That is, a positive deviation in investment adjusted for trend seems to be associated with a large negative deviation in savings, and vice versa. However, a negative change in savings means a positive change of the same size in anti-savings. Since new income consists of investment plus anti-savings, a deviation in investment will tend to produce a much larger change in the same direction in new income.

The standard deviation of savings is usually several times as large as the standard deviation of investment. Hence the behavior of the rate of saving will in general tend to dominate the behavior of new income, and we may say that, as between the two possible controls over income (by way of savings or by way of investment), it is much more important to stabilize the former than the latter. We may also say, on the basis of the negative correlation revealed optically by Figure 4, that increased saving by society as a whole will produce a cyclical decline in income almost invariably.

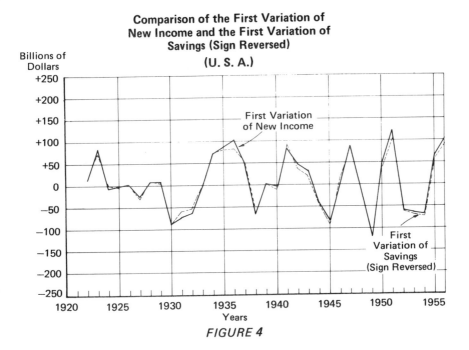

FIGURE 4

Short-run fluctuations in the new income of the whole economy are almost entirely controlled by the variation of anti-savings. The truth of this statement is verified by Figure 4, wherein we have plotted the data for the first differences of new income and the first variations of anti-savings. The correlation between the two curves is astonishingly high, and the correlation coefficient is +.97.

Scarcely any part of this ultra-high correlation can be said to be "spurious," because there is no secular auto-correlation in either time series in the chart, and there is only a little cyclical auto-correlation. Nor is the nearly perfect correlation due to the fact that we are dealing with identities. A degree of freedom for each monthly value in each series is gained by the fact that the first variation of new investment appears in the identity involved, *viz.*

$$I \equiv \gamma - \sigma \qquad\qquad 5{:}18$$

$$dI \equiv d\gamma - d\sigma. \qquad\qquad 5{:}19$$

It is, of course, very true that anti-saving is included in new income, but the two variables do not *have* to be correlated perfectly, because they are not identities.

Chapter 6

FLUCTUATIONS IN TOTAL WAGES

In Chapter Two of this work we announced our intention to employ fluctuations in the total flow of funds as our "reference cycles," and to explain fluctuations in most of the important economic aggregates in terms of this multi-dimensional and multi-faceted variable—the total flow of funds in exchange for services and tangible goods. The special problem of the present chapter is to evaluate total wages (and salaries) as a function of $Z(t)$, which may be regarded either as the rate of total sales of services and tangible goods or as the rate of total purchases of services and tangible goods, valued at market prices as of the moment of sale or at cost price to the buyers.

In Chapter Three it has been shown that the rate of increase of tangible wealth valued at cost, which is of course equal to the difference between the rate of cost of and rate of output of services and tangible goods, is also equal to the rate of investment $\gamma(t)$. The rate of total output of services and tangible goods is, of course, the same thing as $Z(t)$, the total rate of purchases of the same items. Hence, we may write the following equation:

$$\gamma(t) \equiv Z(t) - E(t), \qquad\qquad 6:1$$

where E represents the rate of total cost, or total expense. As is more convenient at present, this formula can be transposed to read

$$Z(t) \equiv E(t) + \gamma(t). \qquad\qquad 6:2$$

The rate of expense, $E(t)$, may be divided into two parts—the expense of labor and the expense of things other than labor. Thus

$$Z(t) \equiv E_1(t) + E_2(t) + \gamma(t), \qquad 6:3$$

where $E_1(t)$ is the rate of labor expense and $E_2(t)$ is the rate of expense of things other than labor at the moment t.

The non-labor expense is chiefly for goods consumed in the productive process, including depreciation of fixed assets. Disregarding taxes and contractual interest paid for the services of capital, practically all of the non-labor expense is for tangible goods, and so, for the sake of simplicity of expression in the analysis of this chapter, the non-labor expense will be referred to as "goods expense." With the help of this abbreviation, formula 6:3 may be translated to read as follows: "Input of labor and goods equals expense of labor plus expense of goods plus investment." In general, expenses do not equal output because investment is not usually equal to zero.

On the other hand, the total rate of *sales* of labor and goods by all traders in the economy is always exactly equal to the total rate of purchases of these items. A wage payment by A (or purchase of labor by him) is a sale of labor by B, and a sale of tangible goods by C is a purchase by D, and so on. Algebraically stated, this fact enables us to write the equation

$$Z(t) \equiv \theta(t) + U(t), \qquad 6:4$$

where $\theta(t)$ is the instantaneous rate of purchase of labor (or rate of payment of total wages) and $U(t)$ is the instantaneous rate of purchase of things other than labor or, for short, the rate of purchase of tangible goods.

It is obvious from an inspection of equations 6:3 and 6:4 that the total rate of expense of labor and goods can be equal to the total rate of purchases of these things only when $\gamma(t) = O$: that is, when there is no investment. It should also be obvious that in any case the rate of purchase of labor and goods includes the rate of investment because

$$Z(t) \equiv \theta(t) + U(t) \equiv E_1(t) + E_2(t) + \gamma(t). \qquad 6:5$$

Furthermore, for society as a whole, sales equal purchases at any time. Hence, when the total rate of sales of labor and goods is broken down into wage payments and purchases of "goods," no term needs to be added to take care of the rate of investment because it is subsumed exactly in the other two terms, as shown by formula 6:5.

Let Z_0 be the money value of the total rate of sales of a certain kind of good, or a certain combination of goods and labor services, at a given instant of time, while W_0 is the value of labor services being purchased at that time for the purpose of replacing Z_0.[1] And let Z_1 represent the value of tangible goods being bought at the same time for the purpose of replacing the values lost by the sales Z_0. Then we may write the following equation:

$$Z_0 \equiv W_0 + Z_1 + d_0, \qquad 6:6$$

The term d_0 represents the amount by which the rate of sale of the first product exceeds or falls short of the value of labor and goods being bought at the given time by the producers of the first product for the purpose of carrying on this productive activity. The subscript, *1*, is placed on the second Z in equation 6:6 to indicate that this quantity of funds is being expended for a stream of goods at a stage of the industrial organization one step removed from the stage at which the sales Z_0 are being made, although they represent the flow of a stream of related economic activities.

The sellers of the stream of goods priced by Z_1 use some of the resulting income to become buyers of labor and purchasers of still other goods one more step from the "original" stage at which the goods priced by Z_1 were sold. Hence the value of the flow of funds represented by Z_1 may be expanded to read

$$Z_1 \equiv W_1 + Z_2 + d_1, \qquad 6:7$$

in which the significance of the terms should be obvious from that of

---

[1] Note that we do not call W_0 the labor *cost* of the goods sold and evaluated by Z_0, but rather something appreciably different.

the analogous terms in equation 6:6. In similar fashion one may write

$$Z_2 \equiv W_2 + Z_3 + d_2 \qquad\qquad 6:8$$

and so on.

Thus the flow of funds at stage zero in this particular complex of productive activity may be "cross-cracked"—to borrow a term from the technology of petroleum—into labor values and "goods" values through a number of stages of the exchange mechanism until the part of the value of Z_O not accounted for by the payment of wages or the difference term, say Z_{r+1}, becomes practically zero, provided only that the series of Z values is convergent.

The ultimate convergence of $Z_{1, 2, 3 \ldots s}$ is indicated by the fact that while Z_S may increase spasmodically, the general drift of Z_S must be downward as the original Z_O is split repeatedly into two parts. For the Z_S values not to converge eventually, the d_s terms, or the difference between sales and purchases for replacement, would have to be consistently negative throughout a "chain" of cross-cracking. This is a highly improbable situation because it would mean that most traders in the given concatenation of productive activity were depleting their funds in connection with this activity and were making up the deficit in funds from another form of traffic in services and tangible goods. For the whole economy, or for the average chain of activity, this result is impossible. On the average, the chains must converge, for otherwise there would be an infinite number of significant stages in the production of some commodity, which is absurd.

By substituting 6:8 in 6:7 and this result in 6:6 and so on, the following matrix is obtained:

$$
\begin{aligned}
Z_0 &\equiv W_0 + W_1 + W_2 + \ldots + W_r + d_0 + d_1 + d_2 + \ldots + d_r \\
Z_1 &\equiv \qquad\quad W_1 + W_2 + \ldots + W_r + \qquad d_1 + d_2 + \ldots + d_r \\
Z_2 &\equiv \qquad\qquad\quad W_2 + \ldots + W_r + \qquad\qquad d_2 + \ldots + d_r \\
&\ \vdots \\
Z_r &\equiv \qquad\qquad\qquad\qquad\ \ W_r + \qquad\qquad\qquad\qquad d_r
\end{aligned}
\right\} \; 6:9
$$

Thus, the wage payment W_r will *tend* to be multiplied several times, so to speak, in the price of the "final" product, while the wage payment W_1 will *tend* to appear twice in the exchange process, contributing directly to the replacement of the value of a commodity one stage removed from the final product and indirectly to the replacement of the value lost by the sale of the "final" commodity in stage zero.

Let $s = 0, 1, 2, 3 \ldots r$ represent the subscripts of Z, W, and d as stated by the set of equations 6:9. Then at the point of convergence, at which $Z_{r+1} = 0$, the summation of the equations in the set 6:9 produces the following abbreviated result:

$$\sum_{s=0}^{r} Z_s = \sum_{s=0}^{r} (S+1) W_s + \sum_{s=0}^{r} (S+1) d_s \qquad 6:10$$

$$= \sum_{s=0}^{r} SW_s + \sum_{s=0}^{r} W_s + \sum_{s=0}^{r} Sd_s + \sum_{s=0}^{r} d_s. \qquad 6:11$$

Other series of sales may be developed, starting with other producers as the zero stage of the pattern of exchanges (or broadly speaking, the pattern of production), whose total money value could be labeled Z_0, Z_0'', and so on. For each such series, an equation like 6:11 will eventually obtain, which expresses each as a weighted sum of wage rates and of differences such as d_s' or d_s''.

The process of generating concatenative patterns of the flow of funds into labor and "goods," respectively, can be continued until every sale of labor and of tangible goods has been counted once, and only once on the left side of equations comparable to 6:11.[2] When the process of generating equations similar to 6:11 has been finished, the grand total of all the equations will be given by the following expression:

$$\sum_{i=1}^{n} \sum_{s=0}^{r_i} Z_{s,i} = \sum_{i=1}^{n} \sum_{s=0}^{r_i} SW_{s,i} + \sum_{i=1}^{n} \sum_{s=0}^{r_i} W_{s,i}$$

$$+ \sum_{i=1}^{n} \sum_{s=0}^{r_i} Sd_{s,i} + \sum_{i=1}^{n} \sum_{s=0}^{r_i} d_{s,i}, \qquad 6:12$$

where $i = 1, 2, 3 \ldots n$ is the number of chains of production in the whole economy.

We recognize the double summation on the left side of equation

---

[2] If the generation of a new series happens to coincide with the first stage of a concatenation already developed, the numbering of the stages can be altered suitably and the two chains or patterns merged into a single one.

6:12 as our "reference cycle," Z, which represents the total sales of services and tangible goods in the whole economy. The rest of the notation may be abbreviated so that the cumbersome expression of formula 6:12 will read as follows:

$$Z = \Sigma \, SW + \Sigma \, W + \Sigma \, Sd + \Sigma \, d. \qquad 6:13$$

All of the variables in this formula are continuous functions of time and could be so expressed explicitly, but this notation has been omitted at present, for the sake of convenience.

The last of the four sums on the right-hand side of equation 6:13 is identically equal to zero. Each individual d term is simply the difference between sales of labor and goods and purchases of labor and goods at a given point in the pattern of the flow of funds at a given time. For the whole economy with all stages included, sales equal purchases identically, and hence the sum of the difference terms, $\Sigma d \equiv 0$.

Moreover, it is very probable that the third of the four terms on the right-hand side of formula 6:13 is also equal to zero because of certain statistical considerations.[3] Hence formula 6:13 reduces to the following expression:

$$Z = \Sigma \, SW + \Sigma \, W. \qquad 6:15$$

Formula 6:15 shows that the total sales of labor and all other goods (not counting intangibles) can be expressed as a mathematical

---

[3]The proof of this statement runs as follows:

$$\Sigma \, sd = \Sigma \, \dot{s}\dot{d} \qquad 6:14$$

where s and d are the deviations of s and d from their respective arithmetic means. This is due to the fact that $\Sigma d = 0$ and $\bar{d}$, the arithmetic mean of the d's is likewise zero. Furthermore, $\Sigma \, \dot{s}\dot{d}$ is likewise equal to zero for the whole economy.

The d terms must converge to zero for reasons already explained. Moreover, they must *average* zero because their sum is equal to zero. If the d's are plotted against the proper values of s, it will be seen that the only way the d's can both converge to and average zero is for the regression of d on s to be zero. Since this is true, the correlation coefficient between d and s is likewis zero. If the linear correlation coefficient connecting two variables is zero, then the sum of the cross-products of their values expressed as deviations from their means is also equal to zero. Therefore, $\Sigma \, \dot{d}\dot{s} = 0$, and from formula 6:14 above we conclude that $\Sigma \, sd = 0$.

function of the total (current) value of wages being paid and the number of stages of production in the established pattern of exchanges of labor and goods throughout the economy. This equation may be revised to read as follows:

$$Z = \left[\frac{\Sigma\,SW}{\Sigma\,W}\right] \cdot \Sigma\,W + \Sigma\,W. \qquad 6:15a$$

In this expression the bracket term is recognized as a weighted average of the number of stages of production in all of the various patterns, where the number of each stage is weighted by the wages being paid at that juncture in the economy.

Let the character m represent this weighted average number of stages of production and let $\theta(t)$ be the value of the rate of total wages and salaries being paid at the moment t. Then formula 6:15 may be revised to read as follows:

$$Z(t) = m(t)\,\theta(t) + \theta(t) \qquad 6:16$$

$$= (m + 1)\,\theta(t), \qquad 6:17$$

where m is still a variable function of time. Now let the value of $m(t)$ increased by 1.00 be represented by $\mu(t)$. Then formula 6:17 reduces to

$$Z(t) = \mu(t)\,\theta(t) \qquad 6:18$$

or

$$\theta(t) = \frac{Z(t)}{\mu(t)}. \qquad 6:19$$

The variable μ is recognized as a wages multiplier, and it will be seen that it has no dimension. In other words, μ is not a dimensional operator but rather is a pure number or coefficient by which the total rate of wages must be multiplied in order to arrive at a figure equal to the total rate of sales of services and tangible goods. From a statistical point of view, μ would be the explicit variable: i.e., it can be estimated from observational data by rearranging formula 6:18 to read

$$\mu(t) = \frac{Z(t)}{\theta(t)}. \qquad 6:19a$$

We have applied formula 6:19a to evaluate μ for the period of 36 years which we are using to verify our theory, and the results are shown in Table 8.

TABLE 8

VALUES OF THE WAGES MULTIPLIER BY YEARS IN THE UNITED STATES

Year	Wages Multiplier μ	Year	Wages Multiplier μ
1921	6.60	1939	6.80
1922	6.24	1940	6.86
1923	6.52	1941	6.82
1924	6.53	1942	6.25
1925	6.84	1943	5.88
1926	6.76	1944	5.84
1927	6.81	1945	5.98
1928	6.98	1946	6.82
1929	7.02	1947	7.16
1930	7.60	1948	7.06
1931	7.58	1949	6.98
1932	6.91	1950	7.17
1933	6.46	1951	6.98
1934	6.03	1952	6.78
1935	6.46	1953	6.60
1936	6.46	1954	6.61
1937	6.44	1955	6.69
1938	6.23	1956	6.62

It will be noted that there is very little secular trend in the value of μ over this particular period of years. It has an average value of 6.65. This means that the average number of stages of production in this country was one less than 6.65, or 5.65, since $m \equiv \mu\text{-}1$, by definition.

One would expect that $\hat{m}$, the average number of stages of production through all manufacturing would be less than the average for all productive activity, because the extractive stage and the wholesaling stage are missing. (Retail operations were designated as the zero stage and hence are not counted in the computation of m.) We can test this deduction by studying the data for a limited number of years in manufacturing industry. In order to eliminate cyclical variations, which probably would cause slightly erroneous estimates of $\hat{m}$, we have chosen to compute $\hat{m}$ by the use of ten-year averages of the total value of product and of total wages paid in the manufacturing industry. These results are shown in Table 9.

The average value of $\hat{m}$ (that is, the truncated value of m) is 3.65, or just two less than the value of m (6.65 - 1.00) for the whole economy, which is about what one would expect. However, the calculation of a wages multiplier by simple division, as in Tables 8 and 9, assumes that the "chains" of production are all convergent and, of course, they are not all convergent in the area of manufacturing alone. We have to confess that Table 9 gives only a blurred estimate of the number of stages of production in the manufacturing industry. We offer the results for what they are worth, and we take some satisfaction in noting that they are all significantly smaller than the value of m for all industry.

The calculated values of the number of stages of production in manufacturing does not vary much over the years. The range of variation is 0.3, which is slight when compared with the average value for the whole period of more than 20 years. This long-term value, as we have said, is 3.65.

TABLE 9

VALUES OF THE WAGES MULTIPLIER IN MANUFACTURING
IN THE UNITED STATES

Year	Ten-Year Averages of the Value of Product in Manufacturing ($\hat{Z}$) (Million Dollars)	Ten-Year Averages of Wages and Salaries Paid in Manufacturing ($\hat{\theta}$) (Million Dollars)	Normal Value of Wages Multiplier in Manufacturing $\hat{\mu}$
1914	19,904	4,291	4.6
1919	36,112	7,719	4.7
1921	43,772	9,851	4.4
1923	55,867	12,667	4.4
1925	57,567	12,913	4.6
1927	58,597	13,116	4.5
1929	60,107	13,498	4.4
1931	59,581	13,261	4.5
1933	53,748	11,822	4.6
1935	50,367	11,059	4.6
1937	49,996	10,809	4.6
1939	47,342	10,095	4.7

The data are from the biennial *United States Census of Manufacturing.*

This comparative stability in the ratio of value of product in manufacturing to wages paid has been observed by other writers, but it has not been explained satisfactorily.[4] On the other hand, our theory supplies a rather satisfactory explanation of the stability of this ratio. Since the ratio is approximately equal to the average number of stages of production, or one more than this number, it would seem that the sheer inertia of a pattern of production embracing thousands of industries and millions of firms would tend to stabilize the pattern.

The average wage per person employed is given, of course, when total wages are divided by N, the number of workers employed, *viz.*

$$W(t) = \frac{Z(t)}{\mu(t)\,N(t)} \qquad\qquad 6:20$$

wherein *W* is the average wage rate per person employed. Fluctuations in average wage may therefore be reported on a proportional basis by this relationship:

$$\frac{dW}{dt}\cdot\frac{1}{W} = \frac{dZ}{dt}\cdot\frac{1}{Z} - \frac{d\mu}{dt}\cdot\frac{1}{\mu} - \frac{dN}{dt}\cdot\frac{1}{N}\, . \qquad 6:21$$

Thus the proportional rate of change of the average wage rate per person is governed, proximately or immediately at least, by just three variables: the proportional rates of change of (a) the total flow of funds, (b) the wages multiplier (or average number of stages of production increased by one), and (c) the number of workers employed. Other things equal, the average rate of wages will increase if the total flow of funds is increased and will decrease if either the number of stages of production or the number of persons employed is increased.

Does formula 6:20 prescribe an "iron law of wages"? Not quite. What the formula does say is that labor unions cannot increase the average wage of *all* employees (including the non-unionized), while holding employment constant, unless they operate in a favorable environment in which either new income is positive (perhaps as a result of large federal deficits, for example) or else the number of

[4]See Simon S. Kuznets, *National Income and Its Composition,* I, p. 227. National Bureau of Economic Research, New York, 1941. See also Sidney Weintraub, *A General Theory of the Price Level, Output, Income Distribution and Growth,* p. 15 *et. seq.,* Chilton, 1959.

stages of production is decreasing. The last-named factor is rather stable and, in any case, is not readily susceptible to collective bargaining. The success of labor unions in raising average wages would therefore seem to depend upon a favorable movement in the flow of funds, to which of course they may contribute in some degree by their cost-push effect on prices or by their direct political impact upon government spending. This direct impact may become especially formidable in election years.

It is interesting to speculate on the significance of formula 6:17 at the limit where there are no "stages" of production for exchange, and all production is carried out on a purely "domestic" basis, so to speak. In that case there is no wage contract in the legal sense of the term. But we can think of individual producers as paying themselves a "wage" for their own productive efforts. Then $m = 0$, and formula 6:17 becomes

$$Z = \theta\,(0 + 1) = \theta. \qquad\qquad 6:22$$

In other words, the value of the product is equal to the *current* value of the effort being put forth to produce it. In general this value is not equal to the labor *cost* of the goods now being consumed, and formula 6:17 cannot be labeled a labor *cost* theory of value. In a modern economy the rate of labor cost would generally be taken to refer to the rate at which wages were paid at some time prior to time t, whereas both Z and θ are evaluated in formula 6:17 as of the present moment, $t = \tau$. And the rate of wages paid at an earlier time will usually be less than the rate at the present moment in a progressive economy. This positive difference in the whole economy is of course a function of the rate of net income being earned by tangible capital, and this for traders as a whole is the same as the rate of new investment $\gamma(t)$, as we have shown.

We now proceed to develop our theory of total wages in terms of total new investment and total rate of conservation of capital (or savings). To do this, we first recall the basic formula given in Chapter Three for the relationship of total capital to total flow of funds, *viz.*:

$$Y_\tau \equiv \int_{\tau\text{-}K_\tau}^{\tau} Z\,(t)\,dt . \qquad\qquad 3:1$$

In this formula Y_T is the value of total tangible wealth at time $t = \tau$ and K_T is the historical period of turnover of total wealth at the same time. $Z(t)$ is, of course, the total rate of purchase of services and tangible goods. We next substitute in this formula the value of Z given by formula 6:18, which gives us

$$Y_T \equiv \int_{T-K_T}^{T} \theta(t)\, \mu(t)\, dt. \qquad 6:23$$

Differentiating this equation we find that

$$\gamma(t) \equiv \frac{dY}{dt} \equiv \left[\frac{\partial Y}{\partial Z} \cdot \frac{\partial Z}{\partial \theta} \cdot \frac{d\theta}{dt} + \frac{\partial Y}{\partial Z} \cdot \frac{\partial Z}{\partial \mu} \cdot \frac{d\mu}{dt} \right] + \frac{\partial Y}{\partial K} \cdot \frac{dK}{dt}. \qquad 6:24$$

Since $\dfrac{\partial Z}{\partial \theta} = \mu$ and $\dfrac{\partial Z}{\partial \mu} = \theta$, formula 6:24 may be restated as

$$\gamma(t) \equiv \int_{t-K}^{t} \mu(t) \frac{d\theta}{dt}\, dt + \int_{t-K}^{t} \theta(t) \frac{d\mu}{dt}\, dt + \sigma(t), \qquad 6:25$$

because the last term on the right-hand side of formula 6:24 is recognized as the rate of conservation of capital or, if you please, by our hypothesis the rate of saving. Transposing and applying the theorem of the mean to the two integrals in formula 6:25, we get the following:

$$\gamma(t) - \sigma(t) = \mu(\xi)\, [\theta(t) - \theta(t\text{-}K)] + \theta(\xi)\, [\mu(t) - \mu(t\text{-}K)] \qquad 6:26$$

wherein $\mu(\xi)$ and $\theta(\xi)$ are mean values of the respective variables.

We wish to express the rate of new wages as an explicit function of the rate of new investment and the rate of saving. Since the rate of new wages is given by $[\theta(t) - \theta(t\text{-}K)]$, we transpose factors again, with the following result:

$$\theta(t) - \theta(t\text{-}K) = \frac{\gamma(t) - \sigma(t) - \theta(\xi)\, [\mu(t) - \mu(t\text{-}K)]}{\mu(\xi)}. \qquad 6:27$$

Thus the rate of new wages is equal to the rate of new investment minus the rate of saving, divided by the wages multiplier, less a correction factor to take care of the effect of variation in the wages multiplier itself. It is important to note that the sign of savings,

TABLE 10

COMPARISON OF ACTUAL NEW WAGES WITH
THEORETICAL ESTIMATES THEREOF

Year	Actual New Wages (Billion Dollars)	New Wages Estimated From Formula 6:28 (Billion Dollars)
1921	+2.62	
1922	-4.52	
1923	+8.46	
1924	+5.20	+5.35
1925	+4.10	+4.17
1926	+5.12	+5.00
1927	+3.03	+3.05
1928	+2.29	+2.21
1929	+3.31	+3.34
1930	-11.56	-12.55
1931	-20.61	-20.93
1932	-25.71	-24.83
1933	-22.59	-20.64
1934	-9.68	-9.10
1935	+1.25	+1.58
1936	+13.23	+12.77
1937	+16.08	+15.38
1938	+8.29	+7.31
1939	+6.33	+6.52
1940	+5.13	+5.51
1941	+17.37	+15.81
1942	+33.92	+34.43
1943	+45.95	+46.55
1944	+36.25	+35.72
1945	+14.27	+13.00
1946	-2.00	-1.78
1947	+7.86	+8.34
1948	+22.27	+22.40
1949	+10.80	+10.89
1950	+11.43	+11.62
1951	+33.49	+33.45
1952	+32.89	+33.18
1953	+24.99	+24.69
1954	+10.85	+8.77
1955	+15.60	+15.14
1956	+31.19	+31.12

σ (t) in formula 6:27 is negative. This shows once again that the rate of saving has a malevolent effect upon an important variable in the business cycle. If the number of stages of production, m, remains constant so that the wages multiplier is also constant, any increase in total wages must come from new investment, and the new investment must exceed savings.

For the purpose of statistical verification, formula 6:27, which gives the instantaneous rate of receipt of new wages, must be integrated for the duration of the accounting period in which the stochastic variables are usually expressed, namely, a year. If ϵ equals one year, we have the following formula for the amount of new wages received in the year ending at $t = \tau$.

$$\int_{\tau-\epsilon}^{\tau} [\theta(t) - \theta(t-K)] \, dt \doteq \frac{1}{\mu(\xi)} \left[\int_{\tau-\epsilon}^{\tau} \gamma(t)dt - \int_{\tau-\epsilon}^{\tau} \sigma(t)dt \right] - \int_{\tau-\epsilon}^{\tau} \theta(\xi) \left[\frac{\mu(t) - \mu(t-K)}{\mu(\xi)} \right] dt \quad 6:28$$

By utilizing the values for yearly averages of μ given in Table 8 in this chapter as well as the data for savings and investment by years as given in previous chapters, we have calculated values for the right-hand side of 6:28, which may be designated "theoretical" values for new wages in the United States during the period of observation used in this work. By utilizing a part of the same data we have calculated statistical values for the left-hand side of formula 6:28, which may be called the observed or "actual" data for new wages by years. These statistical results are also shown in Table 10, along with the theoretical results. Both the theoretical and the actual values for annual new wages have been plotted in Figure 5. It will be noted that the two curves in the chart are nearly coincident, as they should be according to our theory.

In conclusion it should be recognized that the rate of increase of total wages is of the dimension "dollars per period of time per period of time," while the rate of investment as commonly understood is of the dimension "dollars per period of time." In order to write the one variable as a function of the other, it is necessary to use a dimensional operator in the equation. In doing so it is not possible to use just any dimensional operator. Only the right operator for the given relationship will do.

Thus, in formula 6:24 the variable $\frac{d\theta}{dt}$ is of the dimension of $/(period of time)^2 while the dimension of γ is simply $/period of

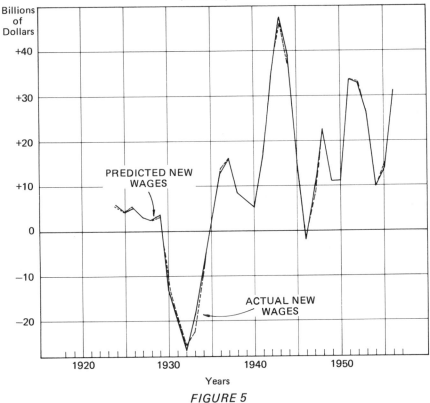

FIGURE 5

time. In the same formula the coefficient $\frac{\partial Z}{\partial \theta}$ has no time dimension, while $\frac{\partial Y}{\partial Z}$ supplies the necessary dimensional adjustment, because this variable is of the dimension

$$\frac{\$}{1} \bigg/ \frac{\$}{\text{Period of time}} = \text{period of time.}$$

This dimension cancels one of the periods of time in the denominator of the dimension of the expression $\frac{d\theta}{dt}$.

Substituting an arbitrary interval equal to a year for the dimensional operator on both sides of formula 6:27 simply will not do the job of explaining the causes of the increase of total wages. We have tried this arbitrary substitution in 6:28 and calculated theoretical and actual values of the increase of total wages from this erroneous equation.   On doing so, we found that there was some degree of positive correlation between the two time series, but the results were glaringly non-identical.

Chapter 7

TOTAL EMPLOYMENT

In the chapter on wages it was shown that the money value of the rate of sale of all services and tangible goods bears a ratio to rate of total wages and salaries which tends to be 1.00 greater than the average number of stages of production in the whole economy at the given time, *viz.*:

$$\frac{Z(t)}{\mu(t)} = \theta(t), \qquad 7:1$$

where Z represents the rate of total sales, θ is the rate of wages and salaries, and $\mu = m + 1$, or the average number of stages of production increased by one.

If we let $W(t)$ represent the average wages being paid per person employed and $N(t)$ represent employment, formula 7:1 may be extended to read

$$W(t) = \frac{\theta(t)}{N(t)} = \frac{Z(t)}{\mu(t)N(t)}. \qquad 7:2$$

This formula may be rearranged to give the number employed at time t as

$$N(t) = \frac{Z(t)}{\mu(t)W(t)}. \qquad 7:3$$

But $Z(t)$ is equal to $M(t)$, the total volume of positively-valued funds, multiplied by $V(t)$, their average rate of turnover in exchange for services and tangible goods.

Let J be the average product per worker per interval of time, measured not in money but in commodities and services, and let

105

P be the average price paid for labor per unit of product turned out by workers, so that, by definition, $J(t) = W(t)/P(t)$. It follows that

$$W(t) = J(t) P(t). \qquad 7:4$$

Substitution of this expression in 7:3 produces this result:[1]

$$N(t) = \frac{M(t) V(t)}{\mu(t) P(t) J(t)}. \qquad 7:5$$

Since μ is an exact function of m, formula 7:5 states the volume of employment at any given time as a dependent of five other aggregates or aggregative averages—the total supply of positively valued funds, their average rate of turnover, the average number of stages of production, the physical productivity of labor, and the average price of labor per unit of product. Brief inspection of the formula shows that an increase in total funds available or in their rate of turnover will increase employment, other things being equal; whereas employment will be decreased by an increase in the number of stages of production, or in the average price of labor, or in the physical product of labor, again other things being equal.

The formula in question may be stated in this helpful differential variant:

$$\frac{N'}{N} = \frac{M'}{M} + \frac{V'}{V} - \left[\frac{\mu'}{\mu} + \frac{P'}{P} + \frac{J'}{J} \right], \qquad 7:6$$

wherein $\frac{N'}{N} = \frac{dN}{dt} \frac{1}{N}$, $\frac{M'}{M} = \frac{dM}{dt} \frac{1}{M}$ and so on. In this form the equation says quite simply that the proportional rate of change in employment is equal to the sum of the proportional rates of change of the aggregative factors in the numerator of formula 7:5 minus the sum of the proportional rates of change of the aggregative factors in its denominator.

If the necessary data were available, we might fit a linear multiple regression equation to the logarithms of N, M, V, μ, P, and J. The

---

[1] The concepts J and P are difficult to define precisely, but they have an intuitive and very real meaning for the layman as well as for the economist. The intricate problem of their precise evaluation will not detain us because no statistical variables are available for J and P for the whole economy.

multiple correlation coefficient between log N on the left-hand side
and the logarithms of all the other variables on the right would be
+1.00, and each partial regression coefficient on the right side of the
equation would be plus or minus 1.00. Then we might define the
elasticity of the demand for labor as

$$e = \frac{\partial \log N}{\partial \log P} . \qquad 7{:}7$$

or the logarithmic *partial* derivative of employment with respect to
the price of labor. Then we would find that $e = -1.00$, which tells us
that an increase of five percent in the price of labor will produce a
five percent decrease in employment *if* all of the other terms in
formula 7:6 remain constant.

However, it is true that the other terms do not usually remain
constant in practice, and the elasticity of the demand for labor is not
negative but positive. A falling price of labor engenders unemploy-
ment because prospective employers as a whole are likely to be in a
pessimistic or recessionary mood at a time when the price of labor is

TABLE 11

SOME VARIABLES IN THE EMPLOYMENT PROBLEM
IN THE UNITED STATES

Year	Number of Persons Employed on a Full Time or Equivalent Basis (Thousands)	Average Annual Wages or Salary (Dollars)
1929	34,863	1,451
1930	32,857	1,417
1931	29,427	1,329
1932	26,022	1,171
1933	25,973	1,077
1934	28,043	1,129
1935	29,033	1,179
1936	30,833	1,235
1937	32,546	1,316
1938	32,007	1,284
1939	33,656	1,318
1940	35,648	1,351

Source: *Statistical Abstract of the United States.*

decreasing. They therefore tend to furlough some labor at such times, and we have a falling price of labor joined with a falling quantity demanded. Similarly, when wages are increasing, the inflationary and optimistic mood of traders causes an increase in demand for the products of labor and an increase in the number employed.

The truth of this observation can be seen in Table 11 which shows the number employed for a period of years together with the estimated values for W, the average price paid for labor per period of time. It can be seen that total employment fell sharply when wage rates were decreasing in the great depression, and that an increase in wage rates in the recovery years was accompanied by an increase in employment.

Notwithstanding the positive correlation between employment and the price of labor in these critical years, there is no doubt that a higher price for labor tends to be associated with reduced employment at any given time. However, any such retarding effect upon employment was more than cancelled in the recovery years by the increase in M, the total supply of funds, which was engineered by the Roosevelt administration by means of its fiscal policies. Even so, the increase of M was held back by congressional opposition to the administration's policy, and no return to "full" employment with rising wages was possible until the outbreak of World War II necessitated the concurrence of Congress in a gigantic increase in the federal debt. This increase stimulated the expansion of credit all along the line and increased M sufficiently to put practically all the able-bodied to work, either in a uniform or without one.

In similar fashion, the Korean War stimulated employment through its effect on the quantity of funds; so also with the adventure or misadventure in Indochina, which has been a support to the level of employment for over ten years. Does war without end contribute a necessary part of a "full employment" federal budget? Perhaps not. If the cities and states were given a share of federal tax and other funds, the door would be opened for a tremendous splurge of inflation, because it would, in effect, give these lower governmental units the power to create funds, acting through their alter ego, the federal government.

In formula 7:6 we have expressed the total number employed as a function of five variables M, V, μ, P, and J, wherein J is a statistical measure of the rate of total product of labor per man per period of time. It will be helpful to set the period of time equal to one year and then express J as the product of χ, h, and a, where χ represents average product per man per hour measured in physical units, and h and a are symbols for the average number of hours worked per man per week and the average number of weeks worked per year. This gives us the following formula for total employment, N:

$$N = \frac{MV}{\mu\,P\,a\,h\,\chi}. \qquad\qquad 7{:}7a$$

The proportional rate of increase (decrease) of total employment is then given by the following:

$$\frac{N'}{N} = \frac{M'}{M} + \frac{V'}{V} - \frac{\mu'}{\mu} - \left[\frac{P'}{P} + \frac{\chi'}{\chi}\right] - \frac{h'}{h} - \frac{a'}{a}, \qquad 7{:}8$$

wherein the primes all indicate rates of change per year.

The bracketed terms indicate, when taken together, the proportionate rate of change of average money wages per man-hour. Including $\dfrac{h'}{h}$ in the bracketed term would formulate average money wages per man-week. From this fact it is seen that, if weekly wages are kept constant while the hours worked per week are decreased, there will be no change in employment because, under the assumed condition

$$\frac{P'}{P} + \frac{\chi'}{\chi} + \frac{h'}{h} = 0, \qquad\qquad 7{:}9$$

and any negative percentage in h will have to be cancelled by positive values for $\dfrac{P'}{P}$ or $\dfrac{\chi'}{\chi}$ or both if weekly wages are to be kept constant.

On the other hand, if hourly wages are kept constant while the average work-week is reduced, there will be a tendency for employment to increase. On an annual basis we might set the normal value of $\dfrac{M'}{M}$ (proportional rate of change in total funds) at about 6 percent, and $\dfrac{a'}{a}$ at about -2 percent, with both rates on an annual basis. We have seen that there is not much secular trend in either direction in μ, the number of stages of production, or in V, the velocity of funds, so the normal changes in these last-mentioned variables may be set at zero. On the assumption that hourly wages are kept constant $\dfrac{P'}{P} +$ $\dfrac{\chi'}{\chi} = O$. We have made an educated guess and placed $\dfrac{a'}{a}$ at -2 percent to take care of the effect of longer vacations. Then the effect on employment of decreasing the work-week from 48 hours to forty hours per week would be given by the following substitutions in 7:8 if we assume that hourly wages are held constant:

$$\frac{N'}{N} = +0.06 +0 - 0 - [0] + 0.18 + 0.02 = +0.26 \text{ or } 26\%. \quad 7:10$$

This result compares favorably with the theory of employment developed by Tinbergen and deWolff. They conclude that a reduction of 18 percent in the work-week would be accompanied by an increase in employment of 26 to 28 percent if hourly wages are kept constant. Their employment model is a great deal more complicated than ours, for they make use of 26 independent variables as opposed to the six in our model.

It should be noted in conclusion that, when $\frac{X'}{X}$ is taken out of the bracket in formula 7:8, it has a negative sign. This means that a decrease in the output of labor per period *tends* to increase employment. So there is scientific support for the intuition of the unions and their leaders to the effect that it is a good thing for workers to impose limitations on their output per man per period of time. There is instinctive truth in the old adage which says, "Whether you work by the piece or the day, decreasing your output increases your pay"— and we might add not only the pay but also the number employed, other things being equal.

Chapter 8

EXPENDITURE OF NEW FUNDS
AND THE PRICE LEVEL

In Chapters Three and Four we showed that the funds to finance new investment do not come from the savings of society as a whole, because of the baleful effect of anti-savings upon the total income of the economy. The funds to finance new investment must come from some kind of economic activity which is not cancelled out because of interaction between individuals and their behavior. Our present task is to seek out and define the source of the funds which provide for an increase of capital, or for new investment, since the two terms are equivalent for all traders taken together.

In tracking down this source we shall continue to use the symbols which were employed in earlier chapters. $Y(t)$ still represents the total value of capital and $Z(t)$ is the rate of total purchases of services and tangible goods, while $K(t)$ is the historical period of turnover of all capital. All variables are expressed as variable functions of time, t. $M(t)$ will represent the total supply of positively-valued funds, while $V(t)$ is the velocity of funds in exchange for goods and services, as defined by the identity

$$V(t) \equiv \frac{Z(t)}{M(t)}.$$ 8:1

It is a common assumption of orthodox theory that every economic man or business firm will try to accumulate as much wealth as possible while maintaining a balance of funds which will satisfy the need or desire for liquidity. The behavior of each individual or firm is therefore presumed to lead to a point of restricted maximization at which the following two equations will obtain simultaneously:

$$\begin{cases} dY_i = 0 & \text{8:2} \\ d(\lambda_i M_i) = 0, & \text{8:3} \end{cases}$$

wherein the subscript i signifies that the formulas refer to an individual and not to the whole economy and wherein λ_i represents a coefficient of propensity to spend. Since formulas 8:2 and 8:3 obtain for every individual in the economy, each formula may be summed in order to change from a point of equilibrium for the individual to a point of equilibrium for the entire society, *viz.*

$$\sum_{i=1}^{n} dY_i = 0 \qquad \text{8:4}$$

$$\sum_{i=1}^{n} d(\lambda_i M_i) = 0, \qquad \text{8:5}$$

wherein $i = 1, 2, 3, 4 \ldots n$ and represents the accumulation of all traders. Furthermore, $\Sigma dY_i = d\Sigma Y_i = dY$ and $\Sigma d\lambda_i M_i = \overline{\lambda}_i \Sigma dM_i = \overline{\lambda}_i \, dM$ if we write $\overline{\lambda}_i$ for an unspecified average value of all the individual coefficients. To simplify the notation we may write $\overline{\lambda}_i$ as λ and the equilibrium point for the whole economy is then specified by the two equations

$$\begin{cases} dY = 0 & \text{8:6} \\ \lambda dM = 0. & \text{8:7} \end{cases}$$

These two equations must be solved simultaneously and, when this is done, we find that the point of restricted maximization must satisfy the equation:

$$dY - \lambda dM = 0. \qquad \text{8:8}$$

When the condition for equilibrium is stated in this way we perceive that λ becomes a coefficient measuring that fraction of additional funds being received which traders as a whole are willing to spend for new investment. Moreover, this fraction is itself equal to the product of the two partial derivatives $\frac{\partial Y}{\partial Z}$ and $\frac{\partial Z}{\partial M}$. The latter of these two gives the value of additional purchases per unit of new funds, and the first gives the value of the new investment produced by the additional purchases, other things being the same. The product of the two stated partial derivatives is therefore equal to λ, the proportion of added funds which traders are willing to spend for additional capital. Substituting this value of λ in 8:8 therefore leads to the solution:

$$dY = \lambda dM = \frac{\partial Y}{\partial Z} \cdot \frac{\partial Z}{\partial M} \cdot dM. \qquad 8:9$$

This formula does not give the value of dY in general, but rather gives its value at the point of equilibrium, which is the value of dY that maximizes the value of new capital for a given amount of funds. The general solution for dY is of course given by

$$dY \equiv \left[\frac{\partial Y}{\partial Z} \cdot \frac{\partial Z}{\partial M} \cdot dM + \frac{\partial Y}{\partial Z} \cdot \frac{\partial Z}{\partial V} \cdot dV \right] + \frac{\partial Y}{\partial K} \cdot dK, \qquad 8:10$$

wherein the letter K symbolizes the average period of turnover of total capital, as always in this work. We may pass from a static equilibrium point to a dynamic situation by dividing 8:10 throughout by dt, differential time, viz.

$$\gamma(t) \equiv \frac{dY}{dt} \equiv \left[\frac{\partial Y}{\partial Z} \cdot \frac{\partial Z}{\partial M} \cdot \frac{dM}{dt} + \frac{\partial Y}{\partial Z} \cdot \frac{\partial Z}{\partial V} \cdot \frac{dV}{dt} \right] + \frac{\partial Y}{\partial K} \cdot \frac{dK}{dt}. \qquad 8:11$$

Substituting a dynamic analog for 8:9 in 8:11 we conclude that, at the point of equilibrium the following relationship tends to exist:

$$\frac{\partial Y}{\partial Z} \cdot \frac{\partial Z}{\partial V} \cdot \frac{dV}{dt} = -\frac{\partial Y}{\partial K} \cdot \frac{dK}{dt}. \qquad 8:12$$

The right-hand side of this formula is recognized as the rate of anti-conservation of capital (or, if one pleases, of anti-saving), while the bracketed expression in 8:11 is another expression for new income. Once again we find that a term equal to anti-savings is concealed in the new income of society so that as before we conclude that saving by society as a whole tends to destroy income, while it has a neutral effect on new investment, as stated by formula 8:9.

The dimensional operator in this formula $\frac{\partial Y}{\partial Z}$, may be replaced by a definite integral, so that 8:9 may be restated as

$$\gamma(t) \equiv \frac{dY}{dt} \doteq \int_{t-K}^{t} \frac{\partial Z}{\partial M} \cdot \frac{dM}{dt} \cdot dt. \qquad 8:13$$

Furthermore the partial derivative $\frac{\partial Z}{\partial M}$ is equal to $V(t)$, the velocity of funds in exchange for services and tangible goods. Hence, 8:13 may be restated in this manner:

$$\gamma(t) = \int_{t-K}^{t} V(t) \cdot \frac{dM}{dt} \cdot dt \qquad 8:14$$

$$= V(\xi)[M(t) - M(t\text{-}K)], \qquad 8:15$$

wherein $V(\xi)$ is an average value of V over the interval of time K. The bracketed expression may be designated as the value of "new" funds at the moment t, and the duration of "newness" is the interval of time K, as it has to be if we are to equate the rate of investment to the rate of creation of new capital. Formula 8:15 tells us that the rate of new investment, $\gamma(t)$, is equal to the value of new funds multiplied by their rate of turnover, or velocity, in exchange for services and tangible goods. It is rather obvious that the product term on the right-hand side of 8:15 should be designated the rate of expenditure of new funds, and we conclude from the formula that this rate of expenditure is equal to the rate of new investment in capital. This in turn means that the source of funds for new investment is to be found in the credit-making machinery, which produces or creates the new funds which are destined to go, directly or indirectly, into the purchase of new capital.

Statistical verification of this theorem can be attempted in two ways. One involves an extensive and indirect approach, whereas the other proceeds by an intensive and direct examination of the pertinent data for the one year in which such examination is possible. The indirect or inferential approach derives from formula 8:11 above, while the direct approach lies in a statistical implementation of formula 8:15.

The bracket term in 8:11 is of course the rate of new income and it is equal to the sum of the rate of expenditure of new funds say

η (t), and the rate of anti-saving, $-\sigma$ (t). Formula 8:11 can therefore be simplified to read:

$$\gamma(t) \doteq \eta(t) - \sigma(t) + \sigma(t) \qquad\qquad 8:16$$

and

$$\gamma(t) \doteq \eta(t). \qquad\qquad 8:17$$

To check the theorem that new investment normally equals the expenditure of new funds (i.e., that $\gamma \doteq \eta$) we may therefore compute the value of η by adding the rate of saving to the rate of new income and then comparing this sum for each year with independent evaluations of new investment, (γ). We have made the calculations for the period of years selected for observation in this study, and the results are shown in Table 12 and also in Figure 6.

TABLE 12

ESTIMATES OF EXPENDITURES OF NEW FUNDS COMPARED WITH
INDEPENDENT ESTIMATES OF INCREASES IN TANGIBLE WEALTH

(Billions of Dollars)

Year	Increases of Wealth	Expenditures of New Funds	Year	Increases of Wealth	Expenditures of New Funds
1922	24.9	23.5	1940	38.3	37.6
1923	31.9	33.7	1941	51.6	52.7
1924	30.8	29.1	1942	68.3	57.7
1925	33.8	32.8	1943	80.6	61.2
1926	35.4	35.4	1944	82.7	67.4
1927	33.1	33.4	1945	80.9	79.3
1928	34.3	34.6	1946	83.2	82.2
1929	39.9	40.0	1947	90.2	87.8
1930	41.6	45.8	1948	104.4	103.0
1931	32.4	33.6	1949	98.6	98.8
1932	17.5	19.1	1950	112.3	112.3
1933	13.1	7.2	1951	128.2	126.3
1934	17.9	7.3	1952	126.8	125.6
1935	23.5	17.0	1953	136.7	136.9
1936	26.7	33.2	1954	123.5	123.9
1937	32.3	33.8	1955	133.1	133.1
1938	28.7	27.3	1956	136.2	135.2
1939	32.4	30.9			

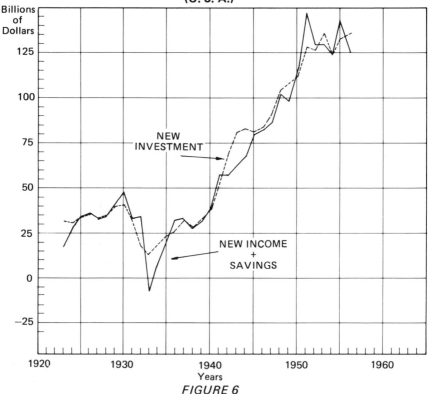

FIGURE 6

Comparison of the two curves shown in the figure shows that they are nearly identical in most years. In fact, the only serious divergence is noted in the years of World War II, when there were many restraints upon investment and traders were not free to maximize their new investment for a given supply of new funds. In other words, the necessary conditions for equilibrium in investment did not obtain, and therefore one should not expect the rate of new investment to equal its equilibrium value, which is the rate of expenditure of new funds.

We proceed to check the theorem of formula 8:15 with observational data for the only period of time for which the necessary data are available, that is to say for the calendar year 1950. As a first step we must convert the instantaneous rates of the formula to the corresponding amounts for a calendar year. If ϵ is an interval of time equal to a year, formula 8:15 may be converted to read

$$\gamma_\tau = \int_{\tau-\epsilon}^{\tau} \eta(t)\,dt = \int_{\tau-\epsilon}^{\tau} V(\xi)[M(t) - M(t-K)]\,dt \qquad 8:18$$

or

$$\gamma_\tau = \overline{\overline{V}}\left[\int_{\tau-\epsilon}^{\tau} M(t)\,dt - \int_{\tau-\epsilon-K}^{\tau-K} M(t)\,dt\right] \qquad 8:19$$

and

$$\gamma_\tau = \epsilon\overline{\overline{V}}\left[\overline{M}_\tau - \overline{M}_{\tau-K}\right], \qquad 8:20$$

where $\bar{V}$ is a moving average value of the velocity of funds in exchange for services and tangible goods, and $M(\tau)$ is the average value of total funds in the given year while $M(\tau - K)$ is the average value during a year (not necessarily a calendar year) ending K years earlier than the end of the given year.

It is desired to show that the total new investment for calendar 1950 is equal to the total expenditure of new funds for that year. The necessary data are available for this year from a study by Dr. John G. Blackburn, which was presented to the University of Florida as his doctoral dissertation in August, 1950. The title of this study is *A Balance Sheet for the Nation: A Study in Concepts.* In this study Dr. Blackburn gives the total amount of positively-valued funds in the United States on December 31, 1950 as $1258.4 billion and on December 31, 1949 as $1152.9 billion.

By a rather intricate manipulation of these two vital benchmarks it is possible to estimate the expenditure of new funds in 1950. We take the simple average of these two observations as the value of M (50), or $1205.7 x 10^9. The average rate of turnover of these funds for the year 1950 is given by dividing this figure into the total sales of services and tangible goods during the year 1950, which amounted to $1036.4 billion. $\bar{V}$ (50) is therefore equal to 0.8596.

Since we have found that, in theory

$$\frac{\partial Y}{\partial Z} \cdot \frac{\partial Z}{\partial V} \cdot \frac{dV}{dt} = -\frac{\partial Y}{\partial K} \cdot \frac{dK}{dt}, \qquad 8:21$$

we draw the conclusion that, at the point of equilibrium, the rate of change of the velocity of funds is inversely proportional to the period of turnover of tangible goods, or directly proportional to their rate of turnover. This leads to the conclusion that $\bar{V}$ (48) = 0.8772, inasmuch as the rate of turnover of tangible goods was slightly higher in 1948 than in 1950. We may then obtain the average total amount of funds for 1948 by dividing 0.8772 into total sales for 1948, which were $939.9 x 10^9. This gives a figure for $\bar{M}$ (48) of $1071.53 billion.

The value of K for 1950 was about 1.95 years. If we assume for the moment a rounded value of two years, the following result obtains

$$\bar{M}(\tau) - \bar{M}(\tau\text{-}K) \doteq \bar{M} \ (50) - \bar{M}(48) \ = \ \$134.12 \ x \ 10^9 . \qquad 8:22$$

The actual value for $\bar{M} \ (\tau) - \bar{M} \ (\tau - K)$ will be a figure slightly less than this, or about $130.77 x 10^9, because K for 1950 was slightly less than two years. $\bar{\bar{V}}$ in formula 8:19 may be taken as the average value of $\bar{V}$ (48), $\bar{V}$ (49), and $\bar{V}$ (50), or an average of 0.8872, 0.8143, and 0.8596, which amounts to 0.8505. The value of $\bar{V}$ (49) was computed on the basis of the same proportionality principle which was used in connection with $\bar{V}$ (48).

We are now ready to make substitutions in the formula for expenditures of new funds in calendar 1950. Substituting the foregoing data in 8:20 we conclude that

$$\eta(50) = \quad 0.8504 \ [\$1205.65 \ -\$1074.88] \ x \ 10^9 \qquad 8:23$$

$$\eta(50) = 0.8504 \ x \ \$130.77 \ x \ 10^9 \ = \$111,200,000,000. \qquad 8:24$$

The total expenditures of new funds in calendar 1950 therefore amounted to $111.2 x 10^9. By our theory this figure should equal the total new investment in the same year. This last figure is of course equal to the difference between the value of total investment on December 31, 1950 and its value on December 31, 1949. Referring to the data given elsewhere for total investment, we conclude that

$$\gamma(50) = Y(12/31/50) - Y(12/31/49) = \$(1,916.3 \ -1,804.2) \ x \ 10^9 . \qquad 8:25$$

$$= \$112.1 \ x \ \$10^9 . \qquad 8:26$$

Hence, the observed difference between total new investment during calendar 1950 and the total expenditures of new funds in that year is given by

$$\gamma(50) - \eta(50) \ = \ \$(112.1 - 111.2) \times 10^9 \ \doteq 0. \qquad 8:27$$

Furthermore the figure for η (50) as obtained by an intensive kind of direct observation for this particular year is in agreement with the inferential value of new investment described at an earlier point in this chapter. If we label the two estimates of expenditures of new funds as η and η', we find that

$$\eta(50) - \eta'(50) = \$111.2 \times 10^9. \ - \$112.3 \times 10^9 \doteq 0. \qquad 8:28$$

Thus the statistical data support the conclusion of mathematical logic, and the assumption that traders seek to maximize their new investment for a given expenditure of funds. Total new investment equals total expenditures of new funds at the point of equilibrium.

It is axiomatic that traders as a whole cannot increase their funds by slowing down their rate of turnover. Rather they must do so by going into fresh debt to themselves, so to speak, and this calls for a type of activity which is different from saving. And the consensus of individual efforts to maximize new investment for given expenditure of new funds will reach an equilibrium point—that is to say, the restricted maximum will be achieved for the whole economy—when the new capital taken as a whole is bought with a total expenditure equal to the expenditure of new funds by society as a whole.

This means that an expanding economy must have a continuous increase of positively-valued funds, which necessitates of course an equal increase in negatively-valued funds. However, it should be understood that this fundamental principle of economics does *not* mean that an inflation of prices is always required in order to create new investment in a less-than-global economy or in a global economy wherein new sources of energy abound. If the supply of goods increases just as fast as the supply of funds, there will be no inflation, i.e., no rise in average prices. The pecuniary evaluation of new investment in this case may be said to represent an equivalent "real" investment. But in any case the supply of funds must increase to permit of new investment and an expanding or "progressive" economy.

The distinction between the pecuniary value of new investment and its "real" value is indeed a crucial problem in the theory of social control, because the behavior of marginal prices is a function thereof, and average prices are in turn a function of marginal prices. Let $Q(t)$ represent a satisfactory measure of the real value of the total stock of tangible wealth. Then $L(t)$, the marginal price level, will be given by

$$L(t) = \frac{dY}{dQ} = \frac{\eta dt}{dQ} = \frac{\frac{\partial Y}{\partial Z} \cdot \frac{\partial Z}{\partial M} \cdot dM}{dQ} \qquad 8:29$$

$$= \frac{CdM}{dQ}, \qquad 8:30$$

where C is a coefficient representing the propensity to spend for new capital. C is, of course, to some extent a variable function of time, although there is reason to believe that it is relatively constant compared with the variation in M because of the tendency for savings to equal the conservation of capital.

Thus marginal prices are clearly determined by the increment of total funds in comparison with the total increment in the "real" value of goods. Since the variation in marginal prices governs average prices, the most feasible point of entry for measures to control prices would seem to be at the point where price increases are generated, and this is in the investment market where new funds are created. Controls should aim to see to it that the total rate of expenditure of new funds (including the expenditures of government) do not exceed the rate at which new "real" investment is being created.

If marginal prices of capital are controlled in the investment market, average prices will also be stabilized. Neglecting the time factor which would cause average price variation to lag behind changes in marginal prices, the average price level, P, would be given by the following formula:

$$P = \int_{Q=0}^{Q} C \frac{dM}{dQ} dQ \bigg/ Q \qquad 8:31$$

$$= \frac{C(\xi) \cdot M(Q)}{Q} \qquad 8:32$$

where $C(\xi)$ is an average value of C. This average value may be safely regarded as a constant in the long run, and we conclude that, in the long run at any rate,

$$\frac{dP}{P} = \frac{dM}{M} - \frac{dQ}{Q}.$$
8:33

This formula tells us that in the long run the proportional rate of change of the average price level is given by the difference between the proportional rate of change in the supply of positively valued funds and the proportional rate of change in the total supply of real wealth. If this conclusion should be derided as only a restatement of the quantity-of-money theory of prices, the answer is "Not quite." In the first place M does not represent the quantity of money but rather a far larger and more pervasive factor, which is the total quantity of positively valued funds. In the second place, our formula for the general price level gives just as much importance to the quantity of goods as it does to the quantity of positively-valued funds.

Chapter 9

GROSS NATIONAL PRODUCT AND THE INVESTMENT MULTIPLIER

The gross national product of an economy would seem to be correctly defined as the pecuniary value of the input of tangible goods and services into the "final" stage of production plus the value of the increase of "capital." The "final" stage is usually thought of as the stage in which goods become "finished"; that is, in which they acquire the time, place and qualitative attributes which enable them to minister "directly" to the health, comfort and satisfaction of the persons who acquire them. This "final" stage would include, of course, governmental services such as the national defense and the national amusement and self-glorification of walking on the moon. The product of the "final" stage includes the "panem et circenses" which all complicated establishments feel is necessary to the prolongation of the establishment.

On the other hand, we demonstrated in Chapter Six that the "final" stage may also be regarded as merely a point of mathematical convergence which can be generated by "cross-cracking" the flow of goods into their antecedent flows at earlier stages of production.[1] This purely quantitative conception of the final stage of production—and therefore the flow of tangible goods and services into that stage—

---

[1] In Chapter Six we pinned the subscript zero on the "final" stage of production and worked "backward" against the flow of services and tangible goods to reach the point of mathematical convergence, which became the r th or "initial" stage. However, the numbering of the subscripts can be reversed, and then the number of the stage at the point of convergence becomes the number of the "initial" stage, while the r th stage of production becomes the "final" stage.

avoids the logical burden of making categorical and arbitrary decisions of a qualitative nature between goods which are in the "final" stage and those which are not.[2]

Qualitative differences give rise to the direction of the flow of goods and services and affect the fluctuations of this flow, but their end results in the aggregate may be handled in a non-qualitative calculus of observations. No doubt a red dress is qualitatively different from a blue dress to a prospective buyer, and a ham sandwich has different vectors of utility from those of a steel rail. However, the physicist finds it more suitable to the scientific evaluation of color to treat distinctions therein as merely variations in a quantitative continuum known as wave-length. In a similar fashion we prefer to evaluate the finality of economic operations in a continuous spectrum of quantitative flows of dollar values without reference to qualitative categories. Whatever may be the qualitative characteristics of goods as they enter the "final" stage of production, they are also entering a stage which is determined by the convergence of a concatenation of a continuous flow of money values, as described in Chapter Six.

As we have shown above, there are on the average m stages of production plus the "final" stage where the goods are bought for personal use, which might be termed the "consumption" stage. But each stage represents the exchange of goods and services, so we may say that there are μ stages of exchange and m stages of production, where $\mu = m + 1$, or, if one pleases, there are μ stages of production and consumption. Also the flow of product into the final stage will be $1/\mu$ th part of the total flow of production throughout all stages. There is, of course, increase of capital in all stages, including the "final" stage, normally speaking. But the part of the increase of capital which is in the "final" or "consumptive" stage has already been counted in the evaluation of the total rate of input into the

---

[2]We do not choose, for example, to be lured into the logical cul-de-sac of trying to determine whether a house is a "producer's good" or not. This question is usually said to be determined by whether it is occupied by the owner or rented out to other parties. We refuse to go along with the usual decision as to whether or when a physician's automobile is capital. Tax law divided the automobile between the two categories. According to the law, when the physician takes his family for a drive in the country, the car is a "final" or "consumer's good." On the other hand, the same vehicle is said to be a "producer's good" when the physician uses it to make a house-call. We prefer not to introduce such metaphysical distinctions into our argument.

"final" stage, which is given by the algebraical expression $\frac{Z}{\mu}$, where Z, as always in this work, represents the total rate of sale of all tangible goods and services. It would therefore be double counting to incorporate the entire increase of capital as a part of the gross national product. The double counting of the increase of capital is avoided by taking a fraction of the increase of capital as a part of the gross national product, where the fraction is equal to the quotient of $\frac{\mu-1}{\mu} = \frac{m}{\mu}$.

In view of the foregoing considerations, the value of gross national product, or G, is given by the sum of $1/\mu$ th of the total flow of tangible goods and services plus a part of the total increase of capital equal to $\frac{\gamma m}{\mu}$. Algebraically putting these two terms together we reach the conclusion that

$$G = \frac{Z}{\mu} + \frac{m}{\mu}\gamma. \qquad\qquad 9:1$$

In this formula, G, Z, and γ are all expressed as dollars per interval of time, while m and μ may be treated as pure numbers.

It is an egregious error to include the gross purchases of all "durable" capital in the concept of gross national product, for this involves multiple counting. If one is to tolerate multiple counting, why not go all the way and define gross national product as the total output in tangible goods and services of all traders, which would make G = Z? Nevertheless the United States Department of Commerce does include the purchases of "durable" capital in its conception of gross national product. This quidnunc or statistical hodge-podge is really the gross national product plus something additional which it is convenient to include in a statistical aggregate which will later become what the Department of Commerce calls the net national product after a capital consumption allowance has been subtracted from it. After further adjustments the gross national product finally becomes equal to the national income, according to the Department.

Statisticians of the Department give themselves a "degree of freedom" in this procedure, which enables them to make the national income derived from gross national product coincide with their estimate of national income considered from the point of view of receipts of money income. This degree of freedom is found in

TABLE 13

COMPUTATION OF THE NET INCREASE OF CAPITAL IN THE
UNITED STATES (BILLIONS OF DOLLARS)

Year	Gross National Product $G(\tau)$	Plow of Funds Divided by Multiplier $\dfrac{Z(\tau)}{\mu(\tau)}$	$G_\tau - \dfrac{Z(\tau)}{\mu(\tau)}$	Estimated Increase of Capital $\gamma(\tau)$
1921	56.4	33.5	22.9	27.0
1922	61.1	37.8	23.3	27.5
1923	70.3	42.7	27.6	32.6
1924	71.1	44.4	26.7	31.5
1925	76.0	48.3	27.7	32.7
1926	80.2	50.3	29.9	35.3
1927	78.5	50.4	28.1	32.9
1928	81.6	52.9	28.7	33.6
1929	85.8	54.6	31.2	36.6
1930	74.2	43.5	30.7	35.9
1931	56.8	35.2	21.6	25.3
1932	41.6	26.9	14.7	17.2
1933	41.1	25.8	15.3	18.6
1934	50.6	29.9	20.7	24.2
1935	56.9	35.9	21.0	24.7
1936	67.0	40.4	26.6	31.4
1937	70.0	43.4	26.6	31.4
1938	65.4	40.6	24.8	29.3
1939	72.8	44.6	28.2	33.0
1940	81.6	48.8	32.8	38.4
1941	104.7	60.3	44.4	51.9
1942	137.7	73.6	68.1	75.0
1943	170.3	91.1	79.2	93.6
1944	182.6	103.1	79.5	95.5
1945	181.2	107.5	73.7	87.7
1946	179.6	116.8	62.8	74.7
1947	197.2	133.3	63.9	75.4
1948	221.6	144.6	77.0	90.9
1949	216.2	140.3	75.6	89.6
1950	240.0	157.0	83.3	97.9
1951	227.0	175.1	101.9	119.3
1952	290.2	187.1	103.1	121.7
1953	302.1	189.7	112.4	131.5
1954	299.0	190.8	108.2	126.6
1955	324.1	201.9	122.2	143.0
1956	353.3	217.9	135.4	158.3

estimating the depreciation of "fixed" capital to arrive at an amount to be deducted from gross purchases of "fixed" capital in order to reach net national product and national income. The actual aggregative amount of such depreciation is, of course, anybody's guess.

With the help of this degree of freedom it is possible to cause the statistical discrepancy, so-called, between the two estimates of national income to be as small as one chooses to make it. Indeed, it would not be necessary to have any statistical discrepancy whatever, except for the fact that perfect agreement between the two evaluations of the national income would seem to be too good to be true and might arouse suspicion on the part of almost any users of the results.

Formula 9:1 for gross national product can be turned around to produce an explicit equation for the net increase of tangible wealth for the whole economy, the value of new investment. This results in the following formula:

$$\gamma = \left[G - \frac{Z}{\mu} \right] \frac{\mu}{m}. \qquad\qquad 9:2$$

This formula shows that the net increase of tangible capital is a function of gross national product, the total flow of funds, and the number of stages of production, m.

This is the formula which we have employed to estimate the increase of tangible wealth by years from 1921 to 1956, to which reference was first made in Chapter Three above. The components of this evaluation of new investment are shown in Table 13. For gross national product, G, we have substituted the national income as reported by the Department of Commerce, because we think that this variable comes closer to our conception of the true value of gross national product. The data shown are not instantaneous rates but annual accumulations thereof, and the coefficients μ are averages for the given years.

Formula 9:1 above gives the value of gross national product as an instantaneous rate with respect to time. In order to estimate the value of net national product it is necessary first to evaluate the rate of national consumption, for obviously the rate of net product equals the rate of gross product minus the rate of consumption. The total rate of consumption is equal to the total rate of expense with all multiple counting eliminated as a matter of common sense. The total rate of expense in all the stages of production, multiple counting included, is equal to the total flow of tangible goods and services minus the rate of increase of capital. And the rate of expense with multiple counting eliminated is equal to the total flow of tangible goods and services less the total rate of increase of capital with the remainder divided by the number of stages of production *and* consumption, which last variable is equal to μ or $m + 1$.

If C is the rate of national consumption, then by our reasoning we arrive at the following formula:

$$C = \frac{Z - \gamma}{\mu}. \tag{9:3}$$

The rate of net national product is equal to the rate of gross national product, G, minus C, the rate of national consumption. By substitution of 9:3 and 9:1 in this expression we conclude that

$$G - C = \frac{Z}{\mu} + \frac{m}{\mu}\gamma - \frac{Z - \gamma}{\mu} \tag{9:4}$$

$$= \frac{m}{\mu}\gamma + \frac{\gamma}{\mu} \tag{9:5}$$

$$= \frac{\gamma.(m + 1)}{\mu} \tag{9:6}$$

$$= \gamma. \tag{9:6a}$$

Thus by our reasoning, the net national product turns out to be equal to the increase of total capital, which is what it should be by common sense.

The "investment multiplier" is usually defined as the number of dollars of gross national product associated with each dollar of new investment, or the ratio of increases in gross national product to increases in new investment. If we let $\hat{\mu}$ represent the investment multiplier, we may then define it mathematically as

$$\hat{\mu} = \frac{G}{\gamma} = \frac{(Z + m\gamma)/\mu}{\gamma} \tag{9:7}$$

$$= \frac{Z}{\gamma\mu} + \frac{m\gamma}{\mu\gamma}. \tag{9:8}$$

Now define $R = \frac{Z}{Y}$ and $\hat{\mu}$ becomes

$$\hat{\mu} = \frac{YR}{\gamma\mu} + \frac{m}{\mu}, \tag{9:9}$$

where R is the average rate of turnover of tangible goods, which is the reciprocal of $\hat{K}$, the average instantaneous *period* of turnover of tangible goods.

Substituting $\hat{K}^{-1}$ for R in formula 9:9 we have

$$\hat{\mu} = \frac{Y}{\gamma\mu K} + \frac{m}{\mu}. \qquad 9:10$$

Moreover, $\frac{Y}{\gamma}$ is the reciprocal of the economic rate of interest, which may be defined as

$$i = \frac{dY}{dt} \cdot \frac{1}{Y} = \frac{\gamma}{Y}, \qquad 9:11$$

or the *proportional* rate at which the value of capital is increasing. Substituting this expression in 9:10 we conclude that

$$\hat{\mu} = \frac{i^{-1}}{\mu K} + \frac{m}{\mu}. \qquad 9:12$$

In other words, the investment multiplier is a function of the economic rate of interest, the wages multiplier, and the average period of turnover of capital. The average value of i during the period of 35 years which are the objective concern of this investigation, the (that is to say) normal economic rate of interest, was 0.044, excluding the years of World War II. The value of i^{-1} was therefore 22.7. The average value of μ was 6.66, which made the normal value of m equal to 5.66. The average period of turnover was 2.52 years. The normal value of the investment multiplier during the period of 35 years from 1921 to 1956 is therefore given by substituting these normal values in 9:12, as follows:

$$\hat{\mu} = \frac{22.7}{2.52 \times 6.66} + \frac{5.66}{6.66} \qquad 9:13$$

$$= 1.35 + 0.85 = 2.20 \qquad 9:14$$

According to our theory of gross national product and net national product, a graph of the annual values of new investment multiplied by 2.2 on the one hand and gross national product on the other should produce two curves whose average values should be about the same and whose ranges are about equal. Figure 7 is drawn in this manner, and it is obvious at once that the observational data meet the theoretical requirements as to overall performance. Even more significant is the fact that the two curves are approximately the same in *every* year outside of the period of World War II.

This last is, of course, just another way of saying that the observed values of the investment multiplier in the United States are approximately constant from year to year, disregarding the dislocations caused by a major war. And this in turn means that we have a statistical *bonus,* so to speak, in the verification of our theory. That is, our theoretical value of the investment multiplier is verified not only in the over-all behavior of the actual data—which is the minimum requirement—but even in the annual values. Through depression, recession, and prosperity, every dollar of new investment in the United States tends to generate in any given year about $2.20 in gross national product.

If the observed values of $\hat{\mu}$ had not been approximately constant from year to year, this would not in itself have invalidated our theoretical estimate of the value of the investment multiplier. However, when the observed values of this multiplier turn out to be nearly constant from year to year, and these individual and constant values are found to be equal to the average value predicted by theory, this constitutes a much stronger verification of theory than would be shown by an equivalence of actual and theoretical values merely with respect to central tendency and range over a period of years.

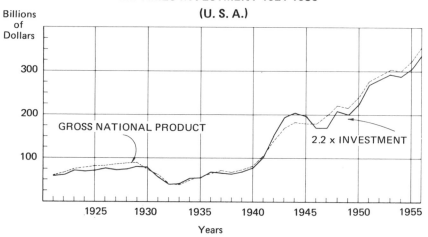

COMPARISON OF NATIONAL PRODUCT WITH
2.2 TIMES INVESTMENT 1921-1956
(U. S. A.)

FIGURE 7

Chapter 10

CONCLUSIONS AND APPLICATIONS

Our analysis has shown that the rate of increase (or decrease) in the total wealth of the economy is equal to the rate of new income plus the rate of conservation of capital. In greater detail the rate of increase (or decrease) in total wealth is equal to the rate of investment plus the rate of anti-conservation of capital plus the rate of conservation of capital. Since the rate of anti-conservation of capital is equal to the rate of conservation of capital with the algebraical sign reversed, it also follows that the rate of change in the total wealth of the economy is equal to the rate of investment, or the rate of purchase of new wealth.

The conservation of capital (savings) cannot contribute anything directly toward increasing the wealth of the whole economy. Because the rate of conservation of capital and the rate of anti-conservation of capital are of equal numerical value but of opposite algebraical sign, the rate of change of society's wealth must be equal to zero if the conservation of capital is the only source of change in total wealth. In that case the rate of new income would also be equal to the rate of conservation of capital with algebraical sign reversed, and the rate of investment would, of course, be equal to zero.

The inability of savings or the conservation of capital to contribute anything directly toward changing the total wealth of society is due to the fact that savings are equal to a reduction of output achieved in a certain fashion; that is, by slowing down the rate of utilization of wealth and making it last longer. Any reduction of output accomplished in this manner by some individuals must reduce the input of some other individuals, since one individual's output is another's input in a physical sense. Thus the act of conserving or slowing down the rate of utilization of wealth must react adversely on total input to the same extent that the act produces a reduction of input at some other point in the economy.

The rate of new income of the whole economy is equal to the rate of investment plus the rate of anti-conservation of capital, but this is the same thing as saying that it is equal to the rate of investment minus the rate of conservation of capital (rate of savings). Thus, in our analysis, there is no need for the rate of investment to equal the rate of savings, or for total investment during a year or other period of time to equal total savings. If both of these conditions did obtain in practice, the rate of new income would be equal to zero and the total income of the economy would remain unchanged during such a period. In practice, we have uncovered no years, in a period of 36 years, in which the new income of the economy of the United States was equal to zero.

If the rate of investment exceeds the rate of savings or conservation of capital, the rate of new income will be positive and the total income of the economy will increase in a period of time in which this condition obtains. On the other hand, if the rate of savings or conservation of capital exceeds the rate of investment, the rate of new income will be negative and the total income of the economy will decrease in a period of time in which this is true.

The fundamental relationships between increase of wealth, new income, investment, savings or conservation of capital, and anti-conservation of capital which exist for the whole economy also obtain in general for the individual. The only important exception is found in the fact that it is possible for the individual to increase his wealth through saving (conserving his wealth or making it last longer). That is, he can make the wealth in his possession last longer without necessarily reducing his own input. The adverse effect of his action upon input will be felt by some other individual or individuals. The concepts of new income, investment, conservation of capital, and anti-conservation of capital from the point of view of the individual meet the tests of logical consistency and integrability in relation to the analogous concepts for the economy as a whole.

The same general conclusions were reached when we analyzed the increase of total wealth from the financial point of view or the point of view of the funds which will make such an increase possible rather than from that of the value of the tangible goods and services. We recalled that the rate of increase of total wealth is equal to the rate of investment and decided that, from the new point of view, the rate of investment must be equal to the rate of flow of funds into investment. One possible source of funds for new investment is the flow of *new* positively-valued funds, a second is the flow of funds made available by saving or the conservation of funds, and a third is a more rapid rate of turnover of existing funds.

It appeared from further analysis that changes in the flow of funds which are made available by savings must always be offset or cancelled by opposite changes which occur in the rate of turnover of existing funds. That is, if an individual increases his savings or his conservation of funds he will at the same time decrease the rate of turnover of his given supply of funds. With this cancellation in mind, the rate of investment of the whole economy at any given time is equal to the product of the positively-valued funds which are "new" at the time multiplied by their average rate of turnover during the interval of newness. This proposition may be shortened to read: "the rate of investment of all individuals in the economy (or the rate of increase of tangible wealth valued at cost) equals their rate of expenditure of new funds."

This equality was found to check out completely in the case of the only year for which all of the necessary observational data were readily available. We also derived indirect estimates of expenditures of new funds and compared these with independent estimates of investment or increases of wealth for the whole economy over the period of 36 years covered by our study. We found that the only years in which the expenditures of new funds were significantly different from the increases of wealth occurred during World War II, and these were years in which traders were not free to maximize their wealth for a given supply of funds because of severe governmental interference and control.

Thus the consideration of savings-in-funds (conservation of funds) rather than savings-in-goods (conservation of capital) does not change our basic conclusions. For the economy as a whole the rate of conservation of funds must be numerically equal to the rate of anti-conservation of funds, and the conservation of funds cannot add a single penny to the total stock of positively-valued funds. The whole *net* effect of the conservation of funds upon total business fluctuations is found in the adverse effect upon the new income of the economy.

In our statistical analysis of these various matters, we computed the total wealth of the United States by years from 1921 to 1956. The differences in total wealth from year to year, recognized as "investment," were shown to be positive throughout the period.

Having developed the concept of K in our theoretical analysis, we proceeded to compute its values for the various years of the period. K is an average period of turnover of all tangible wealth and also an "interval of newness" with respect to income. It provides an answer to the question of how new is "new" and how old is "old."

With these materials in hand we were able to compute new income for each year from 1921 to 1956 on the basis of the formula which says that new income for a year ending at time τ will be equal to the total sales of that year minus the total sales of another twelve-month period (not necessarily a calendar year) ending K_τ years earlier than time τ. The figures for new income reflect the cyclical fluctuations in total economic activity in the United States with great fidelity. This result is attributed to the fact that the figures for new income are not first differences in the total flow of funds from year to year but rather show the difference between the total flow of funds in given years and the flow of funds at a variable time in the past, depending on values for K_τ which range from 1.77 to 4.44 years.

Inasmuch as the rate of savings of the economy is equal to the rate of increase of wealth minus the rate of new income, we computed the annual savings of the economy by subtracting new income year by year from the increases of total wealth (or investment). We also computed annual savings. We computed such savings by an independent and more direct method, and showed that the two sets of values for savings tend to have the same algebraical sign and frequently are nearly in agreement numerically.

Total savings were shown to be in almost perfect negative correlation with fluctuations in total business activity because they are almost perfectly correlated negatively with new income. Or, to put it another way, the fluctuations in new income show almost perfect positive correlation with fluctuations in anti-savings (savings with algebraical sign reversed). These results are those which would be expected on the basis of our theory which shows that new income is equal to investment plus anti-savings or investment minus savings.

A fairly large negative correlation between savings and investment adjusted for trend was readily discovered, but the more significant relationship between variations in savings and variations in investment adjusted for trend yielded a correlation coefficient of only -0.55. Nonetheless, a positive deviation in investment adjusted for trend seemed to be associated with a large negative deviation in savings, and vice versa. However, a negative change in savings means a positive change of the same size in anti-savings. Since new income consists of investment plus anti-savings, a deviation in investment will tend to produce a much larger change in the same direction in new income. Increased savings by society as a whole will produce a cyclical decline in income almost invariably. Short-run fluctuations in the new income of the whole economy are almost completely controlled by the variation of anti-savings, and the correlation coefficient between first differences of new income and first variations of anti-savings amounts to +0.97.

We next developed the important concepts of the "stages" of production and exchange and of the "wages-multiplier," and showed statistically the remarkable stability of the wages-multiplier during the years included in our study. The average wage rate per person employed per period of time is equal to the total rate of flow of funds divided by the product of the number of persons employed and the wages multiplier. Other things equal, the average rate of wages will increase if the rate of the total flow of funds is increased and will decrease if either the number of stages of exchange (wages-multiplier) or the number of persons employed is increased. In view of the stability of the wages-multiplier, it is doubtful that labor unions can increase the average wages of *all* persons employed unless they operate in a favorable environment in which the total flow of funds is increasing (a development to which the unions may, of course, be able to contribute through their bargaining or political efforts).

The rate of payment of new wages and salaries is equal to the rate of investment minus the rate of saving, divided by the wages-multiplier, less a correction factor to take care of the effect of variation in the wages-multiplier itself. If the number of stages of production and the wages-multiplier remain constant, any increase in total wages must come from new investment, and the new investment must exceed savings. We calculated the theoretical values for new wages in the United States over the period of years included in this study and found that these values coincided almost perfectly with observed or actual values for new wages.

The volume of employment at any given time is dependent upon five other aggregates or aggregative averages—the total supply of positively-valued funds, their average rate of turnover, the average number of stages of production, the physical productivity of labor, and the average price of labor per unit of product. Other things equal, an increase in total funds available or in their rate of turnover will increase employment, whereas an increase in the number of stages of production, or in the average price of labor, or in the physical product of labor, will tend to decrease employment.

Thus it seems that total employment cannot be taken to be a simple function of national income and production unless a number of other actual variables are eliminated by assumption. Other analyses make use of a much greater number of variables than we do in developing a theory of employment, but it seems likely on limited evidence that our seven-variable model may turn out to be about as useful as the more complicated approaches for purposes of prediction.

Under ideal conditions we would take the elasticity of the demand for labor to be the logarithmic partial derivative of employment with respect to the price of labor, and would expect the coefficient to have a value of -1.00. This would tell us that an increase of five percent in the price of labor will be associated with a decrease of five percent in employment, if all of the other variables remain constant. Actually, of course, the other variables do not remain constant in practice, and the elasticity of the demand for labor appears to be positive rather than negative.

An increase in the monetary value of wealth is not always the same thing as an increase in the quantity of tangible wealth. It is true that an expanding economy must have a continuous increase of positively-valued funds (which necessitates, of course, an equal increase in negatively-valued funds). However, this does not mean that an inflation of prices is always required in order to finance new investment in a less-than-world economy. If the supply of goods increases as fast as the supply of funds, there will be no inflation (rise in average prices), and the pecuniary evaluation of new investment will represent an equivalent "real" investment. But in any case the supply of funds must increase to permit new investment to take place and provide an expanding or "progressive" economy.

We could not leave the question of funds without some comment on their relation to the level of prices. Our analysis indicated that marginal prices are determined by the increment of total funds in comparison with the total increment in the "real" value of goods. If prices are to be stabilized, controls should aim to see to it that the total rate of expenditure of new funds (including the expenditures of government) do not exceed the rate at which new "real" investment is being created. In the long run, the proportional rate of change of the average price level is given by the difference between the proportional rate of change in the supply of positively-valued funds and the proportional rate of change in the total supply of real wealth.

We have developed a new and logical concept of national product (or gross national product) in terms of the flow of services and tangible goods through the "final" stage of exchange in a given year plus the increases in the value of wealth in other stages of exchange during the same period. National product, as defined, must always be identically equal to national income, or the total of payments received for services rendered by the productive agents in creating the national product, without any allowances for double-counting, arbitrary adjustments for the depreciation of capital goods, changes to account for indirect taxes, business transfer payments, and net subsidies, or any other manipulation whatever. The only difference between national product and national income lies in the point of view from which the same transactions are regarded. When the aggregate is viewed as national income, it is seen to consist of payments for labor services and payments for the use of (alias the earnings of) tangible productive wealth, commonly called land and capital goods.

The term "net national product" is reserved by us to mean gross national production minus gross national consumption. If there were no increase of total wealth in a given period, national consumption would equal national production, and net national product would be zero. In such case, the value of the services and tangible goods "used up" in the "final" stage of exchange would be the same as that of the flow of services and tangible goods into the "final" stage. When there is a net increase of tangible wealth in a given period, net national product turns out to be exactly equal to the net increase of total tangible wealth and, of course, to investment (total purchases of new wealth).

The "investment multiplier" is usually defined as the number of dollars of gross national product associated with each dollar of new investment, or the ratio of increases in gross national product to increases in new investment. We concluded that the investment multiplier is a function of the economic rate of interest (the proportional rate at which the value of capital is increasing), the wages multiplier, and the average period of turnover of capital. For the period from 1921 through 1956 this multiplier was found to have an average theoretical value of 2.2. Actual data for investment and national income were plotted on a graph, with the annual values for investment multiplied by 2.2. The two resulting curves, besides having the same average and range, are approximately the same in every year outside of the period of World War II. Thus our concept of the investment multiplier was judged to be valid and realistic.

Many people, including a large number of economists, seem disposed to confuse matters of theory with questions of policy (that is, to confuse explanations with prescriptions). We have no desire whatever to add to such confusion, and our primary object has been to set forth a new theory of business fluctuations. However, there may be no harm in discussing some implications of our work in connection with policy at this point.

If a situation arises in which the total volume of employment is less than we should like it to be, what can or should be done in an effort to increase the level of total employment? From our formula for total employment we could readily conclude that total employment would be increased if we lowered the average price paid to labor per unit of output. And this would be true if we could depend on all other factors in the situation to remain unchanged, but there's the rub.

According to the usual explanation, money wage cuts in depression are likely to be ineffective in increasing total employment because they tend to have an offsetting adverse effect upon the aggregate demand for goods and hence on money prices. From our point of view it would be said that cuts in money wages per unit of product would tend to have an offsetting adverse effect upon the total flow of funds in exchange for services and tangible goods. Moreover, our statistical analysis of the elasticity of the demand for labor has indicated that it may be difficult or impossible in short periods of time to get a significant negative value for this coefficient, so that a cut in wage rates may not be expected to produce an increase in total employment. Thus in a way our analysis tends to support the usual conclusion with regard to cuts in money wages in depression.

In a situation in which the total volume of employment is less than we should like it to be, one would therefore be tempted to fall back on the standard remedy. This involves deficit spending on the part of the federal government in an effort to increase (in our terms) the total flow of funds in exchange for services and tangible goods. This according to our formula, would have the effect of increasing the total volume of employment if all other variables remained unchanged.

It should be remembered, however, that there would be no iron-clad tendency for total employment to increase in this situation unless other things remained unchanged. If previously employed workers, who had been putting in a short work-week, now came to work longer hours per week and if they were able to take advantage of the greater total rate of flow of funds in exchange for services and tangible goods to demand and obtain higher rates of pay per unit of output, who knows what would happen? All or most of the effect of increasing the total flow of funds might be absorbed by changes in these variables, with little or no effect on the total number of persons employed.

Even if these things do not happen, there is no guarantee that deficit spending to increase the total flow of funds in exchange for services and tangible goods will increase total employment to any great extent. Government spending is always likely to have an inflationary effect as well as a re-employing effect, and the inflationary effect is likely to become larger as the economy moves closer to full employment. Unless the induced increase in the total flow of funds is matched by increased output of commodities and services, the effect will be at least in part that goods will swap for increased amounts of funds per unit, and total employment may not rise sharply.

Thus it seems that conclusions concerning the effects of policies designed to increase total employment must always depend upon assumptions that certain actual variables remain inactive. It should also be noted that this is true of the standard conclusion that cuts in money wages in depression will not be effective in increasing total employment. If, for example, the supposedly offsetting declines in money wage rates and prices occurred in depression, lower prices for goods produced in this country stimulated exports, and the increased volume of export trade had a multiplied effect on domestic production and national income, cuts in money wages in depression might be good for total employment. The same thing would tend to be true if cuts in money wage rates and in money prices of goods automatically caused the revenues of the federal government to fall off rapidly, because they were derived largely from taxes levied at progressive rates, while its total expenditures could not be cut nearly so rapidly, could not be cut at all, or actually increased.

As we have noted in part, our analysis does not furnish the basis for a highly optimistic opinion of the ability of labor unions to secure economic gains for all workers. Unions apparently cannot increase the average wages of all members of the labor force unless they function in a favorable environment in which either the total flow of funds is increasing or the number of stages of exchange is decreasing. Because the latter factor is known to be rather stable, the success of labor unions in this matter seems to depend upon a favorable movement of the total flow of funds.

Changes in total wages in the economy are equal to changes in the total flow of funds divided by the wages-multiplier. This relationship will apparently obtain whether or not there is a strong union organization at work. A strong union organization may be able to divert a part of an increase in total wages away from unorganized workers and into the pockets of union members (or their officers) but this does not seem to be a very remarkable accomplishment from the point of view of the economic welfare of all members of the labor force.

Again, our analysis has indicated that new wages in a period of time must be equal to the difference between investment and savings divided by the relatively constant wages-multiplier. Labor unions cannot control either total investment or total savings by direct application of their powers. Total investment is dependent upon total expenditures of new funds, and total savings do not depend upon wages and salaries so much as they do upon investment. Thus new wages are not subject to the direct control of labor demands or of wages received for labor. Investors seem to be the important characters in connection with fluctuations in total wages from period to period.

In view of the various factors which have been considered, it might well seem wise to abandon policies aimed directly at controlling total employment. The alternative would be found in policies intended to control the level of national income, while permitting total employment to shift for itself. When depression threatened, the desire would be to make new income positive, and the longer-range goal would be to keep new income positive and increasing in total amount.

As indicated in Chapter 5, if one could obtain control over the savings of the economy in some fashion or other, one could control almost perfectly the cyclical fluidity of new income and therefore to a high degree the cycles in gross income. However, the nature of a public policy which would afford effective direct control over savings is not readily apparent. Therefore, it seems necessary to approach the problem of control by way of investment.

The rate of new income is equal to the rate of investment plus the rate of anti-savings or anti-conservation of capital. Since anti-savings are only an offset to savings or the conservation of capital, a policy directed at making new income positive would seem to involve an effort to increase the rate of investment or the rate of purchases of new wealth. We have seen that the rate of investment (in monetary terms) is approximately equal to the rate of expenditure of new funds. When the government increases its total expenditures with funds which are not taken away from the private sector of the economy by means of taxation, it tends to increase the rate of expenditure of new funds, (unless there is a strong adverse change in the velocity of circulation) and hence to increase the monetary value of the rate of investment.

Nor is this necessarily all. The variations of savings are negatively correlated with the variations of investment adjusted for trend, and savings have a standard deviation which is several times as large as that for investment. A policy which tends to increase the rate of investment to something over and above the figure which could have been anticipated will tend to decrease the rate of savings, and to decrease also the numerical rate of anti-savings which must be deducted from the rate of investment in order to arrive at new income.

In other words, government spending which tends to increase the rate of investment to a level higher than would otherwise have been anticipated will tend to have a multiplied effect on national income (by way of new income) and a greater multiplied effect on the total flow of funds in exchange for services and tangible goods. However, enthusiasm over this conclusion would be reduced to some extent because the correlation between variations in investment adjusted for trend and variations in savings is not particularly high and because the reaction of savings to investment is simultaneous at some times but occurs with a variable lag at other times.

The policy of deficit spending by the federal government when depression threatens is not an unusual one either in theory or in practice. It is usually recommended in order to furnish offsets to unnecessary savings which the individuals and firms of the economy are determined to make willy-nilly. Our reason for the policy is considerably different, for it is suggested here for the purpose of making new income positive by increasing new income directly and by indirectly reducing savings (which will also have a favorable effect on new income).

It should also be noted that the policy recommendation concerning deficit spending is as open to the indictment of inflationary bias in the one case as in the other. Deficit spending, which tends to increase the rate of expenditure of new funds, operates only on the monetary value of the rate of investment. If an increase in the monetary value of new investment, or of the rate of purchases of new wealth, is unaccompanied by an offsetting increase in the rate at which new articles of real wealth are produced and made available for purchasing, one effect of the government policy will tend to be the inflation of prices. Continuing inflation may turn out to be the cost attached to government policies directed toward the stabilization of national income and employment.

The use of fiscal policy by the federal government is not the only method available for controlling the level of national income by way of the new income of the economy. The rate of new income is dependent primarily upon the rate of investment which is achieved, and the rate of investment (in monetary terms) is approximately equal to the rate of expenditure of new funds. In this connection it makes no great difference whether the rate of expenditure of new funds is changed because of manipulations of government expenditures and revenues or because of changes in the rate at which new funds are made available and expended through the banking and monetary system. In either case the rate of investment (and the rate of new income) will change if there is a change in the rate of expenditure of new funds.

Changes in the rate at which new bank credit is issued tend to produce changes in the rate at which total funds become available and in the rate of expenditure of new funds. This in turn produces changes in the rate of investment, and fluctuations in the rate of savings tend to be inversely related to changes in the rate of investment (viewed as departures from the figures which could otherwise have been expected). Finally, changes in the rate of savings bring about equal and opposite changes in the rate of anti-savings and thus in the deduction which is made from the rate of investment in its influence on new income. Thus changes in the rate of investment tend to have some kind of multiplied effect on the rate of new income and on the rate of national income.

It appears, therefore, that monetary policy, which influences the rate at which new bank credit is made available, is another device for controlling the rate of new income and hence the level of national income. It also appears that, if recommendations for policy were to be made on the basis of our analysis, monetary policy would play a somewhat larger part than it would if recommendations were based upon the standard or Keynesian explanation of fluctuations in total economic activity.

The reasons for using monetary policy are also somewhat different on the basis of our analysis than on the basis of the standard analysis. We do not speak of changing the supply of funds in order to raise or lower the rate of interest in relation to the marginal efficiency of capital and to raise or lower the economy's investment schedule so that the level of national income at which total investment will be equal to total savings will be more nearly to our liking. For us, the control of bank credit and indirectly of the total supply of funds is intended to change the rate of expenditure of new funds and the rate of investment or rate of purchases of new wealth. Then the changing rate of investment is supposed to be associated with a change in the opposite direction in the rate of savings (as defined by us). This will produce another opposite change in the rate of anti-savings, so that the original effect of the change in the rate of investment on the rate of new income will be magnified.

Regardless of policy recommendations and the analyses upon which these recommendations are based, we think that complete economic stability must always prove to be a will-o'-the-wisp, in practice. We have not tried to develop sure-fire recommendations for controlling fluctuations in total economic activity. We believe that our analysis provides a superior explanation of these fluctuations, especially since it is not based entirely upon a priori reasoning but is readily verifiable in terms of observational data for the economy of the United States. And we believe, therefore, that our analysis will provide a more reliable basis than other analyses for any policies which the people and the government of this country may decide to follow in an effort to control fluctuations in total economic activity.

INDEX